Music in Crime, Resistance, and Identity

This book considers the intersection of music, politics and identity, focusing on music (genres) across the world as a form of political expression and protest, positive identity formations, and also how the criminalisation, censuring, policing and prosecution of musicians and fans can occur.

All-encompassing in this book is analyses of the unique contribution of music to various aspects of human activity through an international, multi-disciplinary approach. The book will serve as a starting point for scholars in those areas where there has been an uncertain approach to this subject, while those from disciplines with a more established canon of music analysis will be informed about what each perspective can offer. The approach is international and multi-disciplinary, with the contributing authors focusing on a range of countries and the differing social and cultural impact of music for both musicians and fans. Academic disciplines can provide some explanations, but the importance of the contribution of practitioners is vital for a fully rounded understanding of the impact of music. Therefore, this book takes the reader on a journey, beginning with theoretical and philosophical perspectives on music and society, proceeding to an analysis of laws and policies and concluding with the use of music by educational practitioners and the people with whom they work.

This book will appeal to students and scholars in subjects such as sociology, criminology, cultural studies and across the wider social sciences. It will also be of interest to practitioners in youth justice or those with other involvement in the criminal justice system.

Eleanor Peters is senior Lecturer in Criminology at Edge Hill University. She has a PhD from the University of Bristol. Her main research interests are in the areas of youth and family justice and the relationship between music and crime. She has published in a number of journals including the British Journal of Criminology, the International Journal of Social Research Methodology and the Journal of Social Welfare and Family Law. Her most recent book is The Use and Abuse of Music: Criminal Records published in 2019.

Routledge Studies in Crime, Media and Popular Culture

Routledge Studies in Crime, Media and Popular Culture offers the very best in research that seeks to understand crime through the context of culture, cultural processes and media.

The series welcomes monographs and edited volumes from across the globe and across a variety of disciplines. Books will offer fresh insights on a range of topics, including news reporting of crime; moral panics and trial by media; media and the police; crime in film; crime in fiction; crime in TV; crime and music; 'reality' crime shows; the impact of new media including mobile, Internet and digital technologies and social networking sites; the ways media portrayals of crime influence government policy and lawmaking; and the theoretical, conceptual and methodological underpinnings of cultural criminology.

Books in the series will be essential reading for those researching and studying criminology, media studies, cultural studies and sociology.

Corporate Wrongdoing on Film
The 'Public Be Damned'
Kenneth Dowler and Daniel Antonowicz

Criminologists in the Media
A Study of Newsmaking
Mark A Wood, Imogen Richards and Mary Iliadis

Music in Crime, Resistance, and Identity
Eleanor Peters

Music in Crime, Resistance, and Identity

Edited by
Eleanor Peters

Routledge
Taylor & Francis Group

LONDON AND NEW YORK

First published 2023
by Routledge
4 Park Square, Milton Park, Abingdon, Oxon OX14 4RN

and by Routledge
605 Third Avenue, New York, NY 10158

Routledge is an imprint of the Taylor & Francis Group, an informa business

British Library Cataloguing-in-Publication Data
A catalogue record for this book is available from the British Library

ISBN: 978-1-032-03047-0 (hbk)
ISBN: 978-1-032-03050-0 (pbk)
ISBN: 978-1-003-18641-0 (ebk)

DOI: 10.4324/9781003186410

Typeset in Times New Roman
by KnowledgeWorks Global Ltd.

Contents

Contributors

Justin Boreland is Director of S.O.U.L Media CIC, London.

Lambros Fatsis is Senior Lecturer in Criminology at School of Humanities and Social Science, University of Brighton.

Craig Hammond is Senior Lecturer School of Education at Faculty of Arts Professional and Social Studies, Liverpool John Moores University.

Kevin Hoffin is a Lecturer in Criminology at School of Social Sciences, Birmingham City University.

Kieran James is Senior Lecturer at School of Business and Creative Industries, University of the West of Scotland, Paisley.

Eleanor Peters is Senior Lecturer in Criminology at Department of Law and Criminology, Edge Hill University.

Christopher Waller is Lecturer in Criminology at London South Bank University, School of Law and Social Sciences.

Andrew R. Wilczak is Associate Professor of Criminology at Wilkes University.

Acknowledgements

Many thanks to Lydia de Cruz, Medha Malaviya and Kavitha Sathish for all their help and support.

1 Music in Crime, Resistance, and Identity

An Introduction

Eleanor Peters

The influence of music on the social world is a complex area, drawing on many theories, explanations, and opinions – so much so that it cannot be clearly understood through the lens of only one academic discipline, nor from just a few global regions. While the study of music is better established in some academic disciplines, in others there is either a very narrow focus of analysis, or there is a lacuna. This volume has identified the commonalities and discords in different disciplinary approaches to understanding music as part of everyday life, focusing on aspects of power, politics, identities, and social harms and crime. The unique contributions from authors in the fields of education, criminology, business, philosophy, and sociology are distinctive. This chapter will begin by explaining what music is and why it is an important issue to consider in terms of crime, resistance, and identity and then describe the content of the remaining chapters.

The main focus of the book is on the political and social aspects of popular music. For many people, music is the backdrop (or the foreground) of their everyday life. This volume examines how music can be utilised in terms of resistance, whether that is through music as an expression of political belief, or as a means to oppose the activities of the powerful. Although it may be a form of resistance, music can also be weaponised as a force by the authorities. Music is generally perceived as 'a good thing' (Edwards, 2011), although there have been many harmful uses of music (Johnson and Cloonan, 2008). Music can be a source of unity, bringing people together, but can also be divisive, forcing people apart.

Music in crime, resistance, and identity?

We feel that we understand music when we hear it, by considering the melody and the vocal or instrumental sounds. The performer articulates and communicates, but the transmission of this has to be read and understood by the listener who may decode and construct it differently from the performer and also from that of other listeners (Kotarba, 2009). Additionally, people's opinions differ about what music is and what is musical, and because of this, it is difficult to define. Music is a socially defined set of sounds, and the

DOI: 10.4324/9781003186410-1

way it is operated in this book is to consider music as a concept that helps explain the social and cultural world, including that of the social status of musicians and fans.

If music is difficult to define then how to begin to define crime? The definition of crime is a contested one; while criminologists and lawyers may discuss crime as it is defined by criminal law, there are other approaches that take a more critical look at processes of criminalisation. Some behaviours are criminalised, and others are not, and this is indicative of an unequally ascribed criminal law where only those behaviours that conflict with the interests of the powerful segments of society are defined as crimes (Quinney, 1977). Criminality is as much a culturally loaded label as it is a neutral legal penalty, and strictly perceiving crime as solely those actions that are against the law may miss a whole raft of harms and injustices. This book operationalises 'crime' in a wider sense than to be just what is, or is not illegal, as laws change across time, place, and cultures.

Resistance can be a form of civil disobedience, a way of protesting to persuade those in positions of power to change laws and policies in order to eradicate certain inequalities (Ferrell, 2019). Resistance is an ambiguous term, and it could be potentially violent dissent to the existing order, but equally it can recognise how people resist in often small, non-violent and often undetected ways (Baaz et al., 2016). Definitions of resistance, as per the Centre for Contemporary Cultural Studies (CCCS) in publications such as *Learning to Labour* (Willis, 2016 [1978]) and *Resistance through Rituals* (Hall and Jefferson, 1993 [1976]), theorise that young people exist in a permanent position of opposition to mainstream authority. This has been disputed by many in an age of neo-liberal consumer values, but there are numerous everyday acts of resistance that are important to consider (Scott, 1987). The tools of resistance may take many forms, one of which is the construction and reproduction of songs, music, and the positionality of musicians in these processes.

Identity may refer to how individuals and collectives are distinguished in their social relations with others (Jenkins, 2014). Identity refers to a social category where a person, or a group of people, is labelled through membership with shared features or attributes. Social categories are understood in terms of sets of characteristics: these can be beliefs, morals, or behaviours expected or obliged of members in certain situations – people may have identities given to them even though they may not particularly feel part of that group themselves. Subcultural identity may be a result of identification with a particular musical genre or perceived membership of a particular group (Peters, 2019).

Central to the approach in this book is the use of the sociological and criminological imagination (Mills, 1959; Young, 2011), where everyday phenomena have meaning on a wider level. There are frequent analyses of cultural artefacts in the social sciences, but this is mostly 'concrete' visual art, rather than the ephemeral such as music. Although most music is viewed as a social 'good', there are also social 'harms' that are associated with it, and this collection aims to reflect this juxtaposition by detailing the positive, and at other times problematic, nature of music. The next part of this chapter considers some of the theorists whose work provides the setting for this book.

Consideration of music by social scientists

Cultural studies gained prominence in the UK in the 1970s through the work of the CCCS,[1] sometimes referred to as the Birmingham School. As one CCCS contributor Bradley (1979: 2) argues,

> the problems of what music is, what it 'means', what unifies different practices from different continents or epochs as 'musical' (if anything), what the relationships are between music and other areas of social life (or human practices, or whatever) – these have vexed and tormented a terrifyingly long list of philosophers, critics and social scientists.

There is no space here to go through all of these tortured philosophers and social scientists, but to note a long-established connection between music and academic analyses, from the ancient Greek philosophers, such as Plato and Socrates, to more modern German thinkers, such as Kant and Schopenhauer. However, I would like to focus on some social scientists here, in a very brief discussion of early considerations of the importance of music to the social world and people's cultural lives in the work of sociologists such as Du Bois in the USA and Weber in Europe.[2]

Du Bois's 1903 publication, *The souls of Black folk*, was ground-breaking in its consideration of the social aspects of musical expression. In it, Du Bois examines the spoken oral tradition in what he terms 'sorrow songs' and begins each of the essays in the book with some music and lyrics that survived following slavery. Du Bois (1989: 179) considers the folk songs that emerged from slavery to be 'the articulate message of the slave to the world'. Du Bois is clear that these are not joyous songs, but ones of unhappy people, suffering disappointment and death.

As Du Bois did, Max Weber also played musical instruments, which influenced his interest in the historical sociology of music, publishing *The Rational and Social Foundations of Music* (Weber, 1958). He saw the importance of music as a social and cultural activity but also its part in the growth of capitalism, a focus that was expanded upon by the Frankfurt School theorists, most notably Theodor Adorno, who perceived mass popular music as manipulating people through its production of simple songs with escapist fantasies. He felt that the 'masses [were] deluded into a preference for the very music that degrades them' (Martin, 2006: 60), but avant-garde music could resist the homogenisation that pop music could not (Adorno, 2004 [1970]). Adorno also took issue with the production and consumption of protest songs, believing that it took the 'horrendous' and made it consumable (Brown, 2007).

Marxist interpretations of popular culture continued with the aforementioned CCCS in the 1970s and 1980s, focusing very much on music as part of spectacular youth cultures – subcultures that, the authors felt, were politically resisting the capitalist 'parent' culture (Hall and Jefferson, 1993 [1976]). Cultural sociology and criminology have continued to influence the study of the intersection of the cultural and the social, addressing one of the main themes of this book: how crime and criminal activity is socially constructed. Cultural criminologists such as Ferrell, Hayward, and Young (2008: 2) looked beyond narrow definitions of crime to consider issues of representation, transgression, and power, highlighting how 'cultural dynamics carry with them the meaning of crime'. The structure versus agency argument continued during the 1990s as overtly Marxist approaches lost influence in an era of postmodernist thinking. However, issues of power, representation, and identity remain at the heart of criminological and sociological thinking, and social scientists continue to explore the meaning of music to identity, behaviour, and emotions (for example, Bennett, 1999, 2001, 2013; DeNora, 2000, 2003; Hesmondhalgh, 2013; Ilan, 2014; Bramwell, 2015; Brown et al., 2016).

What this book is about

This book examines how music is used in identity formation, in reputational management, and how music can be a form of resistance. A person may choose to take up membership of a particular musical subculture, and this may be willingly entered into, with the knowledge that your new tribe are socially or culturally 'oppositional'. However, you may not be aware of exactly how transgressive your new peers are and how disreputable mainstream society perceives them. You may also be given a reputation that you cannot easily contest – and perhaps one that involves criminalisation. Musicians and fans of music as diverse as heavy metal and drill may experience this. Issues of resistance to/from and (re)formulations of identity are important because of the way in which musical and subcultural identities are frequently considered as deviant and transgressive and how, for some, this necessitates the creation, articulation, and development of identity in relation to this. Music can be used constructively to assist with positive identity formulation, and identification with musical subcultures can be helpful, whether at an individual level or more broadly in society. Being part of a musical subculture or just being involved in music can be good for well-being, identity reinforcement, and as a vehicle for personal, political, and communal change.

What each chapter covers?

The rest of this book covers four broad areas beginning with consideration of the intersection of music, politics, and identity, focusing on music (genres) across the world as a form of political expression and protest. The next part covers transformative and transgressive identities, looking at how philosophically, through musical listening, we can find complexities, connections, and hope and can evoke renewed visions of different possibilities for ourselves. These identities may sometimes be forged in certain conditions, but with the support of fellow music travellers, a communal identity can be forged. The third section moves away from the positive identity formations that can occur, to that of the censuring, policing, and prosecution of musicians, particularly when those who are in power, or more powerful, decide that music is criminal, blasphemous, or obscene and therefore undesirable. This can result in criminalisation and othering. The final section considers the use of music in the criminal justice system and reflects on the use of music in penal or punishment locations, looking at how music is used (and misused) by prisoners and examines the benefits of music making and production for positive well-being and hope for the future for young people in conflict with the law.

Each chapter in more detail

This volume starts with an examination of music and politics in its more conventional nature. Andy Wilczak highlights the long history of 'protest' music in the USA and its links with social change and in political campaigns. The historical use of protest songs in the civil rights era and specifically around the Vietnam War is considered, but the chapter also looks at more recent attempts at understanding the phenomena of the symbiotic relationship between music and politics, focusing on the Reagan-Bush era through to the recent Black Lives Matters.

Kevin Hoffin then considers the politics of the left and the right in the black metal scene in Norway and questions whether the stereotype and labelling of some of the musicians and their fans as far-right racists is accurate. The connection of black metal to Norwegian identity came to international notice when there was focus on a number of arson attacks on churches in the 1990s. This led commentators to explicitly link 'a frost-bitten nostalgia' for a previous era in Norwegian history with black metal, far-right politics, and Nazism.

Next Craig Hammond takes a more philosophical approach to exploring the meanings in music by considering a sonic philosophical journey. Using the work of Bloch, Deleuze, and Barthes in exploring musical experience, *listening* can become a creative practice, which can encourage subjective, reflexive, and interior responses, and an ability to transcend into an interior world. During this, it is possible to gravitate towards hope and learn how to 'sing new songs for tomorrow'. The patterns of music can suggest renewed visions of different possibilities, and the ability to write ourselves into a utopian text of music that does not yet exist.

Kieran James considers the cultural interpretations of heavy metal in Indonesia, where bands may face the attention of the police because of 'moral panics' about blasphemous t-shirts and perceived satanism in their music. The chapter highlights how a musical festival was cancelled owing to the nervousness of the police in allowing the heavy metal concert to continue. Police and politicians fail to understand the nature of these musical communities, or the subcultural discourses and practices involved, because they are replete with symbolism, and although adapted to suit local preferences is essentially a music genre imported from the West.

The right or desire to express and communicate via music is explicitly examined in Lambros Fatsis's chapter on drill music. Often perceived as dangerous, drill is pursued and processed as such by the police, prosecutors, and judges without interrogating the prejudicial assumptions that lead to its discriminatory suppression. The censuring of the art and the criminalisation of the artists indicates a misunderstanding of the expressive nature of the genre. The chapter considers the perceptions of misogyny and violence that can lead to criminalising rap, while normalising violence in other aspects of life.

Related to this, Eleanor Peters' chapter explores music as a human right. Looking at the use of legislation to ban music, laws across the world which proscribe some music, or types of musicians, it can be seen how restrictions on the activities of female and LGBTQ and other marginalised musicians occur in some countries. Protection of artistic freedom is found in a number of United Nations human rights articles and derogation from this is contrary to human rights laws and conventions. This exemplifies the power struggles between those who are powerful enough to be heard, and those who are not.

Moving on to examine music in the carceral and judicial systems, Chris Waller considers the realities of music, sound, and noise within the prison estate and how music can be a freedom (and a restraint) for those incarcerated. Music is a powerful feature of the collective life of the prison, as it can aid in the identification of shared experiences. In informal contexts, music can provide a range of benefits for prisoners, as music is used to reconstruct and repair one's sense of self which has been suppressed by a custodial identity.

The positive use of music is also explored in the final chapter, where a consideration of musical provision in the youth justice system in England and Wales is illustrated by a conversation between the editor, Eleanor Peters, and the musician, educator, and British Phonographic Institute (BPI) gold record recipient, Justin Boreland. Desistance-based approaches are increasingly being pursued; these encourage policies of rehabilitation, reintegration, diversion, and desistance. Participation in music projects is one example of this approach, and this chapter considers how they have been successfully used with young people in conflict with the law.

Notes

1 Music-centred, post-war youth cultures were of major interest to the theorists of the Birmingham School, most notably authors such as Stuart Hall and Dick Hebdige (Hebdige, 1979; Hall and Jefferson, 1993 [1976]). Frith, a contributor to *Resistance through rituals*, would continue to be influential in the sociology of music (Frith, 1981).

2 A significant influence on sociologist Howard Becker's work on labelling theory was as a result of his involvement in Chicago jazz subculture (Becker, 1963).

References

Adorno, T. (2004 [1970]) *Aesthetic theory.* London: Continuum.

Baaz, M., Lilja, M., Schulz, M. and Vinthagen, S. (2016) Defining and analyzing "resistance": Possible entrances to the study of subversive practices alternatives. *Global, Local, Political, 41*(3), 137–153.

Becker, H. (1963) *Outsiders: Studies in the sociology of deviance.* New York: Simon & Schuster.

Bennett, A. (1999) Subcultures or neo-tribes: Rethinking the relationship between youth, style and musical taste. *Sociology, 33*(3), 599–617.

Bennett, A. (2001) *Cultures of popular music.* Milton Keynes: Open University Press.

Bennett, A. (2013) *Music, style, and aging: Growing old disgracefully?* Philadelphia: Temple University Press.

Bradley, D. (1979) *The cultural study of music: A theoretical and methodological introduction.* CCCS Special paper no 61.

Bramwell, R. (2015) *UK hip-hop, grime and the city: The aesthetics and ethics of London's rap scenes.* London: Routledge.

Brown, A., Spracklen, K., Khan-Harris, K. and Scott, N. (Eds.) (2016) *Global metal music and culture: Current directions in metal studies.* New York: Routledge.

Brown, R. (2007) *Theodor Adorno on popular music and protest.* Retrieved from https://archive.org/details/RicBrownTheordorAdornoonPopularMusicandProtest. Accessed on June 15, 2018.

DeNora, T. (2000) *Music in everyday life.* Cambridge: Cambridge University Press.

DeNora, T. (2003) *After Adorno: Rethinking music sociology.* Cambridge: Cambridge University Press.

Du Bois, W.E.B. (1989 [1903]) *The souls of Black folk.* New York: Bantam Books.

Edwards, J. (2011) A music and health perspective on music's perceived "goodness". *Nordic Journal of Music Therapy, 20*(1), 90–101. https://doi.org/10.1080/08098130903305085

Ferrell, J. (2019) In defense of resistance. *Critical Criminology.* https://doi.org/10.1007/s10612-019-09456-6

Ferrell, J., Hayward, K. and Young, J. (2008) *Cultural criminology: An invitation.* New York: Sage Publication.

Frith, S. (1981) *Sound effects: Youth, leisure, and the politics of rock 'n' roll.* New York: Pantheon Books.

Hall, S. and Jefferson, T. (Eds.) (1993 [1976]) *Resistance through rituals: Youth subcultures in post-war Britain.* London: Routledge.

Hebdige, D. (1979) *Subculture: The meaning of style.* London: Routledge.

Hesmondhalgh, D. (2013) *Why music matters.* Malden, MA: Wiley.

Ilan, J. (2014) Commodifying compliance? UK urban music and the new mediascape. *Tijdschrift over Cultuur and Criminaliteit, 4*(1), 67–79.

Ilan, J. (2019) Cultural criminology: The time is now. *Critical Criminology, 27,* 520.

Jenkins, R. (2014) *Social identity.* London: Routledge.

Johnson, B. and Cloonan, M. (2008) *Dark side of the tune: Popular music and violence.* Aldershot: Ashgate.

Kotarba, J.E. (2009) "I'm just a rock 'n' roll fan": Popular music as a meaning resource for aging. *Civitas – Revista de Ciências Sociais [Civitas – Journal of Social Sciences], 9*(1), 118–132.

Martin, P.J. (2006) Music, identity and social control. In S. Brown and U. Volgsten (Eds.) *Music and manipulation: On the social uses and social control of music.* Oxford: Berghahn Books (pp. 57–73).

Mills, C.W. (1959) *The sociological imagination.* New York: Oxford University Press.

Peters, E. (2019) *The use and abuse of music.* Bingley: Emerald.

Quinney, R. (1977) *Class, state, and crime: On the theory and practice of criminal justice.* New York: David McKay.

Scott, J. (1987) *Weapons of the weak: Everyday forms of peasant resistance.* Paperback. New Haven: Yale University Press.

Weber, M. (1958) *The rational and social foundations of music.* Carbondale: Southern Illinois University Press.

Willis, P. (2016 [1978]) *Learning to labour: How working class kids get working class jobs.* London: Routledge.

Young, J. (2011) *The criminological imagination.* Cambridge: Polity Press,

2 Revolutionary Music and American Protests

Four Dead in Ohio

Andrew R. Wilczak

Revolutionary music and American protests

This chapter will examine the role of music in protests in the United States, focusing specifically on music produced and protests that occurred during the Civil Rights era (1948–1963), the Vietnam era (1963–1975), the administration of Presidents Reagan and George H.W. Bush (1980–1992), President Clinton and President George W. Bush (1992–2008), and the administration of Presidents Obama and Trump (2008–2020). Note that the administration of President Jimmy Carter is excluded from the conversation not to cast a kind light on his administration or to disparage him in any way, but simply because it doesn't feel like his time in office should be combined with either the conclusion of the Vietnam era or the rise of Reagan's America. The author invites and encourages separate analysis focusing on any and all protests that may have emerged between 1977 and 1981 directed specifically at President Carter.[1]

The sociology of revolutions

There are essentially three ways to think about revolutions and revolutionary movements; from the top-down: a structural-functionalist approach, a Marxist/historical-materialism approach, and a more movement-specific case study kind of approach. For our purposes here, we're going to think about music and political violence in the United States in terms of all three approaches, though, I think we can make a very strong argument that both the Marxist/historical-materialist approach and the structural-functionalist approach ultimately arrive at similar conclusions, and even take very similar paths to arrive at their point.

We will start with the easiest theoretical application for our purposes: the case study approach, where focus is on the events of a singular revolutionary period without considering how it may or may not be similar to other revolutions. This has largely been the primary way of teaching and learning about revolutions in the United States – that to understand the events of the American Revolution, we focus on the political and

DOI: 10.4324/9781003186410-2

social events of that period alone. It is the narrative model of understanding revolution, a historical storytelling with little attention paid to any larger sociological analyses. For instance, a case study approach to the American Revolution would focus on the events leading up to 4 July 1776: the consequences of the Seven Years' War between England and France, colonial determination to expand westward, and 'no taxation without representation'. It would focus on the violence specific to the Boston Massacre and the property destruction in the Boston Tea Party. That Washington, Jefferson, Franklin, and the other leaders of the revolutionary generation were in positions of power prior to the revolution is often presented as a fait accompli.

Moving above the case study approach, we find the two titans of classic sociological theorizing: structural functionalism on the right, conflict theory, here in the guise of historical materialism, but still Marx and Marxism underneath the costume, on the left. Historically speaking, we've been able to find these theoretical perspectives and their respective political ideological offspring at loggerheads, no matter what the issue is. In analyzing the sociological causes of revolution, these perspectives draw very similar conclusions, and the key difference between them is in how much emphasis is placed on the role of economic disruption and/or economic change as a cause of revolution.

From the Marxist perspective, historical materialism is the fuel driving all revolutionary action (Skocpol 2015). Historical materialism views human behavior as defined by labor and the means of labor available. As societies grow and evolve technologically, there is eventually a point of no return wherein technological development clashes with pre-existing, 'traditional' economic norms. This conflict ultimately reshapes and redefines labor both in theory and application, which in turn changes the existing social and political order of a society (Skocpol 2015).

The functionalist approach to revolution is a little more complex, at least in terms of the number of factors that contribute to revolution. First, the key point of agreement: the economic conditions of a society absolutely do contribute to revolutionary action (Johnson 1982). Not only can it launch otherwise obedient, law-abiding people into a career of violence and protest, but it can also tamp down those impulses – in other words, if there are other things driving revolutionary action, a strong economy may limit the ability of those would-be revolutionaries to accomplish their goal. Besides economic factors, the functionalist perspective on revolution also argues that revolutionary violence stems from both the ability of government to meet the most basic demands of its people: essentially, food, water, and shelter (Johnson 1982), though we could argue that in the 21st century this may include electricity, fuel, and internet access. The functionalist perspective on revolutions also argues that the ability of society to integrate with its natural surroundings plays a significant part in this as well (Johnson 1982). One example is if a government is unable to manipulate or otherwise reasonably control nature (from cities dealing with local topography and ecology to federal government management of natural disasters). On the surface, the functionalist perspective really argues that revolutionary violence will only happen if a government is unable to meet these relatively basic demands, which may seem fairly obvious. The real strength of the functionalist approach to revolutionary violence is in the balancing act: we have to weigh economic considerations against so many other factors that predicting revolution and revolutionary violence feels almost as scientific as gambling on professional sports.

We can use the American Revolution as an example again to see the strengths and weaknesses of the functionalist and conflict approaches. From a functionalist perspective, the American Revolution happened because the monarchy no longer met the needs of the colonists; from a colonial perspective, England was no longer concerned with the well-being of the colonies or the colonists. Between the violence in New England, the establishment of forts through the present-day Midwest to prevent westward expansion under the guise of protection, taxes viewed as unjustly hoisted upon the population, and the flat-out refusal by the King and his advisers to hear any of the colonial positions, that the colonies rebelled comes as no surprise. England, and the monarchy, were no longer functioning the way the emerging power base in the American colonies needed them to.

Thinking about the American Revolution in terms of Marxism and historical materialism is a more difficult challenge. To be clear, there absolutely are social and political revolutions in world history where this perspective makes absolute sense: in France and Russia, for example, examining these revolutions with an eye toward the economic infrastructure of those societies is vital. In the American context, the Marxist explanation of revolution runs into some challenges as the Marxist approach to revolutions challenges us to look at the economy of a society and whether and how it butts up against the existing political systems. If there is a significant and enduring conflict between economic and political forces, then a revolution occurs to reshape the political structure to suit the needs of the economic one. In the American context, there absolutely was a conflict between economic forces and the monarchy, but nothing that rose to the level of becoming the dominating factor in the revolution. The conflict over taxes was not strictly economic – this was about the philosophy of liberty and freedom of self-governance, not just the inability of some colonists to pay these taxes. There is no major technological innovation in this period that is being hindered by the monarchy. The slave trade is still going strong, driving the economic engine of the colonial. The conflict between England and the colonies is over industrialization, as England attempted to block colonial expansion westward out of fear of significant industrial growth pushing the colonies towards independence. Here, economic conflict is not a direct catalyst of revolution.

Criminology and revolutions

Mainstream criminological theory has had little to say about political violence and social upheaval, though that isn't to say it cannot be applied. We can certainly consider music a socializing force (Burgess and Akers 1966) and/or a potential coping resource (Agnew 1992), which might in either case teach or reinforce violent norms (Anderson 1999). Most criminological theories were not written with this kind of intentional rule-challenging, system-breaking behavior in mind: if anything, these sorts of theories of crime taught in the United States encourage students to think of the law as an immutable, eternal entity, and those who break it as scoundrels who have lost their way through the valley of righteousness.

This does not mean that no criminological theory has anything useful to say regarding political protest and the crime that may be associated with it, only that we need to use our imaginations to think of ways the majority of theories may apply. Viewing revolution through the lens of family, peer, and community dynamics is certainly one worth exploring in future research. For now, let's focus on those explanations of crime and justice that do account for protest and revolution.

Reactionary and revolutionary suicide

The first major theoretical perspective we can apply to political violence and music is Durkheim's (1897) concept of anomie. Durkheim's classic work on suicide gave us the language to explain feeling disconnected from the larger world around us and can be used to connect those feelings of alienation and normlessness to the larger sociopolitical world to actions that we would typically associate with political protest, violence, and revolution. Essentially, Durkheim argues that feeling disconnected from the society one lives in can result in a downward spiral leading to death by suicide. We can expand Durkheim's conceptualization beyond suicidal behavior to all manner of self-destructive habits – for example, we can view substance use disorders that arise from a sense of anomie as a form of suicide in slow motion.

Less clear is how, from Durkheim's original conceptualization of anomie, a connection can be made between self-destruction resulting from a sense of normlessness and involvement in political protest and violence. In his book *Revolutionary Suicide*, Huey Newton (1973), co-founder of the Black Panther Party, distinguishes between what he calls revolutionary and reactionary suicide. Newton argues that Durkheim's vision of anomie points to a set of reactionary behaviors – that these responses to feeling normless and alienated and out of place are to draw inward, wilting like a flower. Revolutionary suicide, according to Newton, is the realization that one cannot abide by this sense of normlessness and the decision to fight to remake the world, even if the odds of victory are impossibly low, even if the likelihood of being killed in the process is almost certain.

The connection between anomie and involvement in political protest, violence, and revolution, should be clear when viewed through the lens of revolutionary suicide. We can look at both successful and unsuccessful political and social revolutions throughout the history of the world in this way – that the cumulative disadvantage of generations of real or perceived oppression reach a boiling point – causing some people, the leadership of these revolutionary generations, to step up and fight back (Sampson and Laub 1997). This is certainly how Newton perceived himself and his peers in the Black Panther Party as well as others involved in the Civil Rights struggle.

Anomie is one of the most versatile explanations we have of social and political revolution. Framing this violence – especially violence that is sustained over decades – in terms of one's inability to accept the current norms and structure of society gives us insight into both the minds of the revolutionaries and the restrictive if not oppressive nature of the governments and societies they are rebelling against.

Structural strain theory

Merton's (1938) structural strain theory offers a more conventional approach to criminological theory and political crime, though certainly not that different from what Newton (1973) would argue decades later, his work is best viewed as a midpoint between reactionary and revolutionary suicide. We should also note that Merton's theorizing was happening at the tail-end of a period of incredible social and political upheaval in the United States, following approximately 50 years of protests by socialists, anarchists, and the labor unions, and multiple combinations thereof, ultimately resulting in the creation of the policies known as the New Deal by President Franklin Roosevelt. Merton's understanding of crime is undoubtedly a result of living his intellectual life during this period.

That said, structural strain theory views crime as an outcome of one's orientation to the dominant sociopolitical culture of society. Specifically, structural strain theory views crime as an adaptation to the American dream; when a person does not value either the culturally defined goals (material wealth) or the institutionalized means of achieving those goals (hard work in legitimate arenas), then they are likely to be involved in crime. Regarding political violence and revolution, Merton's typology of possible adaptations to American culture included rebellion, which he defines as simultaneously accepting and rejecting both the cultural goals and institutionalized means of obtaining those goals. In other words, there is something about the core of society that rebels want to change – their simultaneous acceptance and rejection of the goals and means is a desire to be treated equitably and a rejection of larger forces oppressing them.

Because it is part of the lineage of anomie, it should come as no surprise that structural strain is also extremely useful in explaining revolutions and provides insight into both the revolutionaries and their oppressors that simply viewing these events through the lens of functionalism or historical materialism.

Critical criminology

Occupying a wholly different space than the Durkheimian tradition of anomie, critical criminology has at its core an innate distrust of the establishment: definitions of crime, enforcement of the law, and the logic of much of what we think of as mainstream American criminology. There is a healthy distrust of authority in this school of thought, and while it is perfectly acceptable to distrust authority in many circumstances, the issue with critical criminology is that the theoretical principles put forward are extremely difficult to test, which is part and parcel with the theoretical perspective at large.

It is difficult to define any singular explanation of crime from the critical school of criminology. In short, crime is socially constructed in a way that benefits the ruling elite. The criminal justice system is a form of oppression used more to protect wealth and property than to actually dispense justice. Quinney (1977) argues that the criminal justice system is a tool used by those in power to maintain their status and dominance over the rest of society. In the eyes of critical criminology, the route to creating justice is through changing the state apparatus. If the justice system exists primarily to serve the property rights of the ruling class, then to create a truly just world at minimum the existing system needs to be de-coupled from property rights and the powers that be held accountable for crimes they have committed; but beyond that, critical criminology would have us question the necessity of many laws to determine whose interests they best serve: the community or the people profiting off of the community.

On the surface, critical criminology seems an obvious fit for the sociology of revolution, and indeed both the critical perspective in criminology and in the sociology of revolutions draws heavily on the work of Karl Marx. The key difference is that Marxist Criminology considers typical offending behavior – simply violating the law and defying state authority – as revolutionary. How this defiance of state authority will create revolution remains to be seen, because there is nothing concerning the relationship between the dominant economic and political structures.

As DeKeseredy (2022) correctly notes, critical criminology has grown beyond the work of Marx in a variety of ways, some of which can help better understand how revolutionary movements occur as well as the role of music (and art more broadly) in these movements. Specifically, narrative criminology (Presser 2013; Presser and Sandberg 2019) provides us with an interesting framework to understand the role of music in revolutionary movements. Narrative criminology examines how stories both create meaning around and influence behavior, including behaviors that could inflict harm. As music is one of the art form that helps inform the narratives of the audience and provides meaning to human life, narrative criminology encourages us to start thinking of music as something that influences the stories people create in and around revolutionary movements and how it might further future action both inter- and intra-generationally.

Beyond narrative criminology, there are further ways critical criminology has developed that are useful to understand the relationship between music and social movements in more specific contexts. While the focus of this chapter is on the evolving Civil Rights movement in the United States, ideas from Indigenous criminology and Southern criminology may help provide meaning to these stories in movements around the world, while both Indigenous and Queer criminology may help further clarify this relationship in the United States. The point of this is to say that critical criminology has, to the credit of the many scholars carrying on this tradition, drawn attention to the multitude of ways people who are not white, cis-gendered, heterosexual colonizers are oppressed and controlled by state apparatuses around the world.

Music and revolution

Having defined the major theoretical perspectives explaining protest, political violence, and revolution, the next step is to explore how these theoretical processes can give us new understanding of the music being created during the periods outlined above. Each period is unique in American history; in the sense that we can think of it as a generation of (mostly) young people dealing with social and political injustice and trying to communicate their dissatisfaction, frustration, and alienation – their anomic feelings (Durkheim 1897; Newton 1973) – in a way that helps create clarity of message, recruit new people into the cause, and perhaps simultaneously cope with the stress of oppression and alienation (Agnew 1992) while also receiving the encouragement and empowerment to fight back against it (Newton 1973).

'Strange Fruit': The Civil Rights era

Beginning with what is commonly thought of as the Civil Rights era (1948–1963) almost seems arbitrary, when we think of both the evolution of music and of sociopolitical protest and violence as both growing out of the work of previous generations. We certainly cannot understand the music of the

Civil Rights era without acknowledging the importance of music among the enslaved Black population of the United States before the Civil War. The use of music as a method of spreading news, a spiritual outlet, and a way to communicate routes along the Underground Railroad, among other things, is absolutely necessary to understand both the origin of the protests during this period as well as the importance of the music created during this time.

Revolutionary music in the Civil Rights era is overwhelmingly spiritual, framing resistance to racial oppression either actively perpetuated or passively accepted by the government as a challenge that one can overcome through sheer perseverance and persistence. As we'll see, this is the only time in the mid-to-late 20th century where spirituality is central to the music of revolution and resistance.

We can also think about music during this period as revolutionary for the simple fact that it existed. As the functionalist perspective on revolutions argues, revolutions begin because a government isn't fulfilling its most basic duties to its citizens. That so many popular artists were singing directly to racial inequality can't be interpreted as anything other than evidence of a breakdown in the function of government. In truth, we could devote an entire chapter to the music of this era, bookended by Billie Holiday's 'Strange Fruit' in 1954 and Nina Simone's 'Wish I Knew (How It Would Feel to be Free)' in 1967 and James Brown's 'Say It Loud (I'm Black and I'm Proud)' in 1968.

What makes this particular brand of revolutionary music interesting and unique from those that followed it is its intense spirituality. This is righteousness in the face of an unholy and unjust oppression, a theological good versus evil manifest on Earth. This is very much a Mertonian (1938) kind of rebellion, an acceptable of the premise of the American Dream but a rejection of the dehumanization of institutionalized white supremacy, without quite rising to the point of Newton's (1973) revolutionary suicide – Civil Rights music is naming the evil, but not explicitly calling for or otherwise emboldening retaliation against it. I suppose, then, that this is an era of resistance: there is less willingness to submit to racial violence and accept it as the norm, but there is also no outward revolutionary tone. At least, not in the music – there is ample historical evidence on the pull between nonviolent resistance preached by Rev. Dr. Martin Luther King, Jr., and the sort of 'by any means necessary' violent revolution championed by Malcolm X. Music that championed a more violent resistance to the cornucopia of oppressive structures in the United States was still a generation away.

'I ain't no fortunate son': The Vietnam era

While music pushing back against racial inequality in the Civil Rights era is very spiritual, music directed at the Vietnam War is less so. Note that there is considerable overlap in these eras, but two significant differences warrant the inclusion of the Vietnam era as its own piece in these analyses: (1) the Vietnam War lasted longer than the Civil Rights movement (essentially, the Civil Rights era ended – or goes dormant – in 1964 with the assassination of Dr. Martin Luther King, Jr. while the Vietnam War continues until 1975, and (2) the anti-war sentiment was race neutral; in other words, white people were affected by and angry about the war, too. We also need to recognize that, obviously, white support for the Civil Rights movement is tempered by the fact that white people benefit from the failure of the movement. Further, support for the Vietnam War was high among both Black and white people in the United States and degraded over time, for Black people faster than white (Gartner and Segura 2000). We could surmise this difference in decreasing support is due to the Civil Rights movement and the growing recognition among the Black community that the US government did not have their best interest in mind.

Nevertheless, music explicitly directed towards the Vietnam War, or that was significant to soldiers and their families, is distinct enough from the music generated by the Civil Rights movement to warrant its own examination. We can see a similar tone to Civil Rights music in tracks like Bob Dylan's 'Blowin' in the Wind' in 1963, Marvin Gaye's 'What's Going On?' in 1971, John Lennon's 'Give Peace a Chance' in 1968 and 'Imagine' in 1971, to name a few. It would also be remiss if I did not include Arlo Guthrie's 19-minute long 'Alice's Restaurant' in 1967 detailing how an arrest for littering made him ineligible to be drafted, saving him from the war. As mentioned, previously this vein of anti-Vietnam War music strikes a similar spiritual tone to the Civil Rights music of this era, in line with the Hippie counterculture of the time, music that politely suggests imperialist nations try to be friends instead of obliterating each other and ending life on Earth as we know it. In some ways, the more spiritual anti-war music has a sort of naivete to it, a generation of young people waking up to the realities of the empire they live in, shocked to discover the very existence of empire itself.

Vietnam era music also takes a more aggressive anti-war and anti-government stance that we'll see echoed in future generations of revolutionary and protest music, as dissatisfaction with the US government is transmitted from one generation to the next. Bob Dylan's (1963) 'Masters of War' has an anger beneath it that breaks through the surface within the first minute of the song, chastising the US military-industrial complex (that it is on the same album as 'Blowin' in the Wind' is masterful). One of the best examples of this is Crosby, Stills, Nash, and Young's 'Ohio' (1970) chronicling the massacre of students protesting the Vietnam War at Kent State University by the Ohio National Guard. Four students were murdered and nine injured in the shooting, and the massacre created the framework we view all protests through today: not whether the state will kill or injure anyone, but how many.

Perhaps the biggest anti-war song out of this era is 'Gimme Shelter' by The Rolling Stones, if only for their massive popularity at the time. 'Gimme Shelter' is a song about how society is precariously close to war – and peace – at any given time. Mick Jagger and Keith Richards's lyrics pull no punches in this track, there is no metaphor here for the audience to try to parse, and yet they were able to produce a piece of music that seems to have a foot in both worlds; there is a spirituality to Gimme Shelter that offsets its more cynical (or realistic) warnings about the immediacy of violence in society. Ironically, the concert the Rolling Stones held to conclude their 1969 tour – the infamous free concert at Altamont, where concert goers clashed violently with the members of the Hell's Angels who were acting as security for the event – clearly delineates the end of the counterculture movement, the end of the hippies, and the transition into a new period in American cultural history.

'Fuck the police': The Reagan-Bush era

The transition from the Civil Rights/Vietnam War era into the 1980s is jarring, both politically and musically. The Reagan-Bush era feels like a smarter, savvier version of the Nixon administration, all of the same political manipulation and skulduggery dressed up in a ready-for-TV package. Vietnam is over, and the Cold War between the United States and the Soviet Union, waged for nearly four decades, is (unbeknownst to many in the United States) on the verge of ending. There is little to no revolutionary protest to speak of during this period; if anything, this is an era of counter-revolution, of entrenched power pushing back in support of the status quo and against the advances made during the 1960s and 1970s. As the focus of this chapter is on revolutionary protest music, and not counter-revolutionary activism and its various manifestations in popular culture, I am going to leave this mine untapped for future researchers to explore.

Musically, the art generated between the 1980s and early 1990s is beloved by some and detested by others. This completes the death of disco and the birth of rap and hip-hop and the multitude of subgenres therein, the evolution of rock & roll into its own array of subgenres – hair metal, heavy metal, death metal – and the introduction of so-called alternative rock, techno, industrial, grunge, and new wave music, to name a few, coming at various times during the decade. With some significant exceptions, popular music in the 1980s and into the 1990s in the United States is as uninterested in major political or social change as the larger society it existed in. If it were, the Parents Music Resource Centre would have gone berserk.

The Parents Music Resource Center (PMRC), an organization that aggressively worked towards censoring music it considered inappropriate for children, was formed in 1985 by the 'Washington Wives', so-called due to their political connections throughout Washington, D.C. Initially, the PMRC focused on music that it deemed to be sexually explicit, profane, or promoted drug and alcohol use, from a critical perspective, it's hard to view this government intrusion as anything other than the beginning of a prolonged campaign to censor the revolutionary idealism and anti-capitalistic nihilism central in (some) music popular with young people. Of the so-called 'Filthy 15' songs used as evidence by the PMRC of music's role in the erosion of morality, only two – 'Bastard' by Motley Crüe and 'We're Not Gonna Take It' by Twisted Sister – were labeled as too violent for consumption, and of those, Twisted Sister's song on youth rebellion is hardly a call to revolutionary action. What it is, for our purposes, is a sign of things to come from future artists (interestingly enough, in testimony before Congress on the song, Twisted Sister frontman Dee Snider argued that the PMRC misunderstood the song and that it was supposed to depict a cartoonish form of violence) (Grow 2015). For now, 'We're Not Gonna Take It' can be considered as a youth anthem similar in message to the Beastie Boys' 'Fight For Your Right (To Party)' released in 1986: music giving voice, but no direction, to the marginalized youth of the nation.

On the topic of the PMRC, it would be remiss if I did not highlight one of the council's most outspoken critics: Eric Reed Boucher, better known as Jello Biafra, lead singer of the Dead Kennedys, one of the most notorious punk bands of the era, producing songs like 'Holiday in Cambodia', 'California Uber Alles', 'MTV Get Off the Air', and 'Nazi Punks Fuck Off'. In addition to his work with the Dead Kennedys, Biafra also had a successful spoken word career, touring the country to lambast the PMRC and Tipper Gore (wife of Senator, future Vice President, and future Presidential Candidate Al Gore) for the PMRC's pearl clutching moralizing and strong-arm tactics. Biafra was outspoken in his advocacy for musicians and his resistance to censorship; not surprising, given the career arc of the Dead Kennedys prior to the establishment of the PMRC and their anti-establishment mission. In the decades since, Biafra has become more involved in political activism and remains a vocal critic of censorship, though he and the rest of the Dead Kennedys are no longer together.

Possibly the most significant revolutionary development during this period is the evolution of rap and hip-hop. Though this genre first appeared in the early 1970s as a logical progression from disco, raps role in highlighting social problems and acting as a voice of the people really begins in the early 1980s with Grandmaster Flash and as mentioned in the discussion of the PMRC, the anti-police message prominent in what would eventually be labeled gangsta rap at the time was enough to draw the ire of the government and their allied talking heads in the media, creating a moral panic centered on the language used in songs like 'Fuck the Police' by N.W.A., specifically expressing false concern that the violent language used in this style of music would lead to the disintegration of morals in the young people listening to them. Here, we can equate morality with belief in and commitment to the status quo, namely, the state and its exclusive right to violence.

An American idiot: The Clinton-Bush era

While the simmering anger of the anti-Vietnam era may not have translated into the Reagan-Bush era, at least not in the mainstream, the 1990s
into the turn of the century saw anger in music intensify substantially during the administrations of Presidents Clinton and George W. Bush. This
is the rise of grunge, death metal, and gangsta rap. This is the beginning
of a new era of socially responsible and politically active musicians, all of
this against the backdrop of the birth of the internet and a new revolution
in music distribution. What makes this era especially interesting for us is
that we're now nearly two generations removed from the music of the Civil
Rights and Vietnam War eras. This is important in terms of the sociology
and history of revolutions: we know that no revolution happens overnight,
but rather is the result of time and dissatisfaction. The social problems that
inspired music of the previous eras: racial inequality, seemingly pointless
wars – were now magnified by increased class inequality and corporatiza-
tion of American politics.

I made an intentional decision to organize the material in this chapter
around Presidential administrations and decades for ease of presentation
but could very well have structured this chapter around violent clashes that
seem to, if not define entire eras, act as clear defining lines from one era to
the next. For all intents and purposes, the Civil Rights and anti-Vietnam
War era begins to end with the riot at Altamont in 1969. The era that followed – dominated by Ronald Reagan and conservative counterculture –
similarly ends, one could argue, with the Los Angeles riot in 1992 after the
infamous Rodney King trial. In 1991, King was brutally assaulted by four
LAPD officers, and the assault was caught on video. In spite of the video
evidence of their guilt, the jury acquitted the four officers, and Los Angeles
exploded – almost literally – in protest. The acquittal and subsequent riots
set off a national debate on police brutality that continues, unfortunately,
some thirty years later.

Musically, the 1990s produced some of the most interesting and ground-
breaking revolutionary work, in this author's opinion. The artists that were
bold enough to lash out at authority in the late 1970s through the 1980s –
the N.W.A., the Dead Kennedys, among others – found themselves part of
a larger chorus of anti-authoritarian and socially conscious music from a
multitude of genres. 'Zombie' (1994) by The Cranberries was published in
response to the death of two children during the Troubles in Ireland and
the band's attempt to push back against the death of innocents in political
conflict. Folk singer Ani DiFranco released an array of socially conscious
music, especially focused on gender and sexuality, including 'In or Out'
(1992) and 'Untouchable Face' (1996). Probably the most well-known protest musicians of the period were Rage Against the Machine. Practically all
of Rage Against the Machine's discography is sociopolitical in some form
or fashion: 'Killing in the Name Of' (1992a), 'Take the Power Back' (1992b),

'Bulls on Parade' (1996a), 'Down Rodeo' (1996b), and 'Sleep Now in the Fire' (1999b) to name only a few.

What's most interesting about the protest music coming out of the 1990s is that it centered on issues that previous generations have fought about – inequality, race injustice – but without significant military actions driving it. To be sure, the United States was involved in plenty of conflicts overseas, but nothing that set off a massive uproar in the zeitgeist at the time. In fact, though we can look at these conflicts through a lens of American imperialism, that they were unjust, unnecessary, and/or uncalled for, the anger that American militarism inspired during the Vietnam war did not materialize in the same way in the 1990s or beyond. In fact, when Natalie Maines from popular country act the Dixie Chicks criticized then-President George W. Bush and the invasion of Iraq and Afghanistan at a London concert in 2003, the Dixie Chicks were effectively blackballed by a country that was now ferociously, venomously nationalistic.

While the Dixie Chicks were blackballed in 2003, in time, other acts were able to push back against the White House and the new post-9/11 America it was building. For example, Green Day's 'American Idiot' (2004) off the album of the same title lashes out using the popular perception at the time of President Bush's lack of intelligence as its weapon. In fact, the Bush administration and the wars in Iraq and Afghanistan both became incredibly unpopular, with Bush's approval rating among the lowest on his last day in office of any President in recent history (The American Presidency Project 2021), but at no point during the Bush administration (or subsequent Presidential administrations that have maintained a US military presence in the Middle East) has there been any sizable rebellion, much less protest, of American militarism by American citizens.

'Alright, in formation': The Obama-Trump era and Black Lives Matter

The final era of American music and revolution discussed may be the most difficult, only because it is the most recent, and it will be some time before historians, sociologists, and cultural critics can well and truly parse out the effects on American life of both the Obama and Trump administrations. As different as these two Presidents are from each other, at least on the surface, their careers are inexorably linked as the election of one created the political toxicity necessary for the election of the other.

Both Presidents experienced their fair share of protests during their administrations. Occupy Wall Street, the first widespread class-based protest in the United States since the 1920s and the execution of Sacco and Vanzetti, drew attention to income inequality in the United States and popularized the distinction between the 1% (the haves) and the 99% (the have nots). Occupy Wall Street also sought to reduce or eliminate corporate influence on politics. Though Occupy Wall Street was ultimately unsuccessful at eliminating income inequality or corporate influence more broadly, they did restart the conversation among a new generation of activists. Similar to the counter-revolutionary movements of the 1980s, the Obama years were also a time of considerable pushback from conservatives in the United States, largely due to the fact that the President was the first Black President in American history, and the circumstances of his birth were part of a conspiracy championed by his successor, who alleged, incorrectly, without a shred of evidence to support his claim, that President Obama was not an American citizen.

During the Trump administration, the United States experienced a level of sociopolitical activism not seen since the Civil Rights and Vietnam War era. The largest protest in American history, the Women's March, took place the day after President Trump was inaugurated, and set the stage for a combative four years. The Trump administration's pledge to 'drain the swamp' and remove what they believed to be bad faith political actors from positions of influence, in actuality, increased the number and power of those bad faith lobbyists, while also weaponizing the 'culture war' leftover from the Obama administration, blasting dangerous rhetoric and harmful policy toward any individual or group who did not genuflect to the President. Like President Bush before him, the approval rating of President Trump when he left office was among the lowest in modern history, though the key difference between them is that President Bush enjoyed an astronomically high approval immediately after the terrorist attack of 9/11, while President Trump struggled to crack 50% for the entirety of his four years in office (Newport and Saad 2021).

Linking these two Presidents is the next generation of civil rights work in the form of Black Lives Matter and the various movements surrounding racial injustice and inequality in the United States, including the protest of the US National Anthem by former NFL quarterback Colin Kaepernick. From the murder of Michael Brown in 2014 to the murder of George Floyd in 2020, the United States has experienced Black Lives Matter protests in cities, suburbs, and college campuses around the country. While this was a period of tremendous political turmoil, musically speaking, there is not much in the way of revolutionary fervor, especially not during the Obama years, in spite of Occupy Wall Street. In the run up to the 2016 election and then the subsequent Trump administration, there was an increase in revolutionary music, but nothing that cut across social strata the way previous generations had. Those artists who were creating socially and political conscious music include Beyonce, Kendrick Lamar, Killer Mike, Run the Jewels, Childish Gambino, and a Tribe Called Quest, whose performance of 'We the People' at the Grammy awards three days after the 2016 election may be one of the most politically conscious moments in award show history. Perhaps this relative silence by white artists during this time speaks to the hegemony of white supremacy in the United States: socialized to support the military in its endeavors to spread imperialism in the name of

freedom and to believe in the veracity of the American Dream and ham-
strung by corporatized music, perhaps vocalizing dissent was no longer
profitable.

Conclusion

The United States has a fascinating revolutionary history. The American
Revolutionary War, though lauded as the spark of modern democracy
inside the American public school system, was ultimately nothing more
than a liberal bourgeois changing of the guard, in that many of the men in
the revolutionary generation who went on to become major political figures
in the early days of the country would have most likely been major political figures in the 13 colonies anyway. In fact, the revolutionary generations
most overlooked success was their ability to whip the public into a frenzy
about social class inequality between the colonies and England while steer-
ing them away from any critical analyses of or action against the deep and
growing social class inequality that existed between colonies and individual
colonists (Jankovic 2019). We also know that the revolutionary generation
balked at the idea of abolishing slavery, though it clearly was antithetical to
the ideas espoused in both the American Declaration of Independence and
the new US Constitution.

What is really fascinating in terms of American revolutionary history is
less the conditions that led to the first revolutionary war and more the conditions that have been bubbling underneath in the centuries since, especially
in the past 50 years (as of this writing). A country founded on ideals of
liberty, justice, and independence has grown into a bloated imperial theoc-
racy clinging to a parasitic economic system that is destroying the environment while flirting openly with militaristic fascism in the name of security.
Thinking of this in terms of the theories of revolution we discussed earlier
and looking through the lens of popular American music since the 1950s, we
can see anomie bubbling under the surface of an otherwise idyllic American
culture – but this anomie has never truly boiled over.

If we separate historical social and political revolutions from the variety
of theoretical perspectives explaining them, the one unifying factor across
these events is, simply, time. Social and/or political upheaval, absent an
external motivating force (i.e., war, famine, disease), cannot happen overnight because they require years – maybe decades, maybe generations – of
mismanagement, misfortune, insult, apathy, inequity, and discrimination,
in various combinations. The relationship between music and revolution,
then, is not necessarily causal; rather, we can look at the music of different
generations as a sort of revolutionary equivalent of the doomsday clock.
The more prevalent the message, the likelier social and political change is
to occur.

Of course, it is also possible and certainly quite likely that there are
people who find themselves swept up in revolutionary movements because

they're drawn to the music first. What these analyses exclude is music as a beacon for the socially marginalized and politically oppressed. Here, the mere existence of certain forms of music are revolutions unto themselves, at least in an American context. For example, the promulgation of square-dancing classes in American public schools as direct resistance to the popularity of jazz throughout suburban American is a topic that needs to be included in any discussion of the role of music in everyday American life and its connection to either resisting or upholding the status quo of the era.

What, then, are the theoretical takeaways of this chapter? As we move from era to era, Presidential administration to Presidential administration, support for revolutionary acts swinging like a pendulum between significant change and significant counter-revolution. The more politically optimistic of you may suggest that this is precisely how a Democratic system is supposed to work, that this speaks to the gridlock that purportedly makes American Democracy the beacon on the hill it was imagined to be when the country was first colonized. We can see anomie wax and wane from one generation to the next; it intensifies, people organize, there is violence, there is further organization around that violence, and then everything is diffused, somehow. Activists are jailed or assassinated. Politicians lose elections or are assassinated. Musicians become unpopular or are assassinated. The status quo remains.

Undoubtedly, the material in this chapter is worthy of its own book and I encourage readers interested in the relationship between popular music and the sociology of revolutions to further explore this space. I have also inadvertently failed to include major songs or musicians who were of vital importance (or who may be beloved by the readers). There were many, many artists pushing back against the status quo but whose work may never have completely broken through into the public awareness at the time. As the purpose of this chapter is to explore the relationship between music and revolutionary acts, music that is undeniably good but that does not catch on with the American public at large may not contribute to social movements in any meaningful way. I invite future research on the music of specific revolutionary organizations and whether and how certain genres of music helped recruit and inspire their members.

It is impossible to study the sociology of revolutions and not become cynical about the subject matter. Removed from these movements and the eras that spawned them by geography and time, one might not feel disappointed when these proto-revolutionary organizations fail to make meaningful change in their communities. As we progress through history and into sociology, the constant battle drum of oppressive forces in American society becomes deafening, and, as a researcher, the failure of movements to generate change and of artists, in this case musicians, to facilitate that change makes objectively assessing these works impossible.

As I mentioned, trying to understand the consequences of the Trump administration on American society is going to be well and truly impossible for some years, perhaps decades. The damage done by the 6 January insurrection and the unfounded conspiracies around the validity of the election should strike fear into the heart of every academic at every level in every discipline reading this text, and, more importantly, every citizen in every Democracy worldwide.

Note

1 Jimmy Carter was President of the United States from 1977 to 1981 but may be remembered more for his work with Habitat for Humanity in the decades since he left office.

References

Agnew, R. (1992). Foundation for a General Strain Theory of Crime and Delinquency. *Criminology*, 30, pp. 47–87.

Anderson, E. (1999). *Code of the Street: Decency, Violence, and the Moral Life of the Inner City*. New York: Norton.

Burgess, R.L. and Akers, R.L. (1966). A Differential Association-Reinforcement Theory of Criminal Behavior. *Social Problems*, 14, 2, pp. 128–147.

The Cranberries. (1994). 'Zombie' *No Need to Argue* [CD]. London, UK: Island Records.

DeKeseredy, W.S. (2022). *Contemporary Critical Criminology*, 2nd ed. London: Routledge.

DiFranco, A. (1992). 'In or Out'. *Imperfectly* [CD]. Buffalo: Righteous Babe records.

DiFranco, A. (1996). 'Untouchable Face'. *Dilate* [CD]. Buffalo: Righteous Babe records.

Durkheim, E. (1897). *Suicide, A Study in Sociology*. London: Taylor & Francis.

Dylan, B. (1963). Masters of War. *The Freewheelin' Bob Dylan* [vinyl]. Columbia Records.

Gartner, S.S. and Segura, G.M. (2000). Race, Casualties, and Opinion in the Vietnam War. *The Journal of Politics*, 62, 1, pp. 115–146.

Green Day. (2004). 'American Idiot'. *American Idiot* [CD]. New York, USA: Reprise Records.

Grow, K. (2015). *PMRC's 'Filthy 15': Where Are They Now?* Rolling Stone, 17 September. https://www.rollingstone.com/music/music-lists/pmrcs-filthy-15-where-are-they-now-60601/twisted-sister-were-not-gonna-take-it-3-180788/ (accessed 6/1/21).

Jankovic, I. (2019). The American Revolution as the Last European Peasants' Rebellion. In I. Jankovic (Ed.) *The American Counter-Revolution in Favor of Liberty*, pp. 3–18. Cham: Palgrave Macmillan.

Johnson, C. (1982). *Revolutionary Change*, 2nd ed. Stanford: Stanford University Press.

Merton, R.K. (1938). Social Structure and Anomie. *American Sociological Review*, 3, 5, pp. 672–682.

Newport, F. and Saad, L. (2021). Review: Presidential Job Approval. *Public Opinion Quarterly*, 85, 1, pp. 223–241. https://doi.org/10.1093/poq/nfaa061

Newton, H. (1973). *Revolutionary Suicide*. New York: Penguin.

Presser, L. (2013). *Why We Harm*. New Brunswick: Rutgers University Press.

Presser, L. and Sandberg, S. (2019). Narrative Criminology as Critical Criminology. *Critical Criminology*, 27, 2, pp. 131–143.

Rage Against the Machine. (1992a). 'Killing in the name of'. Rage Against the Machine [CD]. New York: Epic Records.

Rage Against the Machine. (1992b). 'Take the Power Back'. Rage Against the Machine [CD]. New York: Epic Records.

Rage Against the Machine. (1996a). 'Bulls on Parade'. Evil Empire [CD]. New York: Epic Records.

Rage Against the Machine. (1996b). 'Down Rodeo'. Evil Empire [CD]. New York: Epic Records.

Rage Against the Machine. (1999a). 'Down Rodeo'. Battle of Los Angeles [CD]. New York: Epic Records.

Rage Against the Machine. (1999b). 'Sleep Now in the Fire'. Battle of Los Angeles [CD]. New York: Epic Records.

Quinney, R. (1977). *Class, State, and Crime: On the Theory and Practice of Criminal Justice*. New York: David McKay.

Sampson, R.J. and Laub, J.H. (1997). A Life Course Theory of Cumulative Disadvantage and the Stability of Delinquency. In T.P. Thornberry (Ed.) *Developmental Theories of Crime and Delinquency*, pp. 133–161. Piscataway: Transaction Publishers.

Skocpol, T. (2015). *States and Social Revolutions: A Comparative Analysis of France, Russia, and China*. Cambridge: Cambridge University Press.

The American Presidency Project. (2021). https://www.presidency.ucsb.edu/statistics/data/final-presidential-job-approval-ratings (accessed 7/5/21).

3 The Norwegian Black Metal Second Wave

A Space for Performative Politics

Kevin Hoffin

Introduction

The Norwegian Second Wave of Black Metal has become an ignomini-ous event in music history; suicides, murders, arson, and far-right political expression have created a viscous shadow from which the genre has never truly emerged from. In many cases, this is due to nostalgia and reverence for the innovators of the scene; the body of work that includes *De Mysteriis Dom Sathanas* (*Mayhem*, Deathlike Silence, 1994), *In The Nightside Eclipse* (*Emperor*, Candlelight, 1994), and *A Blaze in the Northern Sky, Under a Funeral Moon* and *Transilvanian Hunger* (*Darkthrone*, Peaceville, 1992, 1993, 1994). Black Metal appears to celebrate atavism and heralds a return to the 'old ways' (by destroying the new) (Hoffin, 2018) through its mix of music, metaphor, and aesthetics (Hoffin, 2018, 2019, 2020). A subculture that constructs itself with such frost-bitten nostalgia became explicitly linked with far-right politics and Nazism. This chapter will explore how these insidious links have cemented themselves, and how disavowal of the Second Wave as simply a hotbed of Neo-Nazism is both reductive and fallacious.

This phenomenon cannot be fully explained without the deeper investiga-tion into the roots of Norway, as a relatively young Country, that regardless holds the spectre of its ancient cultural history aloft in reverence; and where it intersects with Black Metal's greatest foes: Christianity. This chapter will argue that an obsession with atavism or primitivism is much more central to The Norwegian Second Wave than fascism.

Atavism in Norway: Norway's history with Christianity

The Norwegian Second Wave was an intense proponent of primitive ata-vism. Atavism or primitivism is a term to describe a preference for ancient methods and ways of life over those of contemporary Norwegian society. Norway is a relatively young country having only been recognised as such since 1908. However, the history of settlements and civilisation in Norway is ancient. Only Christianised between the 10th–12th centuries on the third

DOI: 10.4324/9781003186410-3

attempt (by force- at pain of death) by the ruling monarch, King Olaf II. The Samis of the extreme north remained unconverted until the 18th century (Dubois, 1999). The first attempt to Christianise the area now known as Norway was in the early 10th century by King Haakon the Good, after an education in England awakened Christianity in him (Wittman, 1910). This attempt failed spectacularly after it was met with severe unpopularity. The second attempt by Anglo-Saxon missionaries succeeded in converting King Olaf I but no one else. His son, Olaf II, became the monarch responsible for Christianising Norway and received sainthood for his duty (Nordeide, 2007). The Norwegians' resistance to Christianity is still a contentious affair. Didactically, the Old Norse gods promoted the ideal behaviour for a prospective Viking Warrior: bravery, ruthlessness, and strength. The Christians promoted mercy, peace, and forgiveness, diametrically opposed to the Vikings' war-like sensibilities. There is a complete divergence of will, aside from personality traits that they condemn – what the Vikings could learn from Christianity was minimal. Secondly, the Old Norse religion meant a lot more to the inhabitants than this strange foreign religion, borne from the Abrahamic community. The Scandinavians held on to the religion that felt most familiar. In the harsh atmosphere of the Northern Hemisphere, there was little remotely tenable between a religion that spoke of a man born king of the Jews and promoted peace and 'loving thy neighbour' and the livelihoods of the Vikings.

Evidence suggests that the Vikings on their invasions had encountered Christianity and added Jesus Christ to their own mythology (Campbell, 1994). Thus, not replacing their beliefs, but assimilating them instead. Coins have been located which feature Pagan gods and Christ in the same image. As far back as the year 772, the Kings of Norway were allied with the Christians in the war against the Danes. The acts of Charlemagne of France finished this allegiance as it came to pass that he had the relic, Irminsul chopped down and assassinated around 5000 Saxon Lords (Vikernes, 2004). At this point, the Scandinavians split away from the Christians and declared a war which would last for further 500 years.

It is a commonly considered view in Norway among the Black Metal community that due to building their churches on sacred Pagan grounds that Christians showed the Pagans no respect so why should they show respect in return (Aites & Ewell, 2009). This statement is often used to justify the church burnings especially by Vikernes. This lack of respect goes further. Once the Christians had taken over Norway and King Olaf II had murdered all dissenters, the irony of a Christian killing to entice followers to a religion of peace notwithstanding, the remaining pagans were driven underground and decried as Satanists for breaking the second commandment. Norway's experience with Christianity is tumultuous at best, and is partially to blame for the atavistic stance of the Black Metal subculture, whereby they actively recall the days before Christianity held sway.

Atavism in Norway: A declaration of nationalism and allegiance to old Norway

In Black Metal's often impenetrable lexicon there is much in the way of archaic language. References to ancient paradigms and myths and in many cases, the bands' native languages. The message of Black Metal is often not encompassed wholly in the lyrics themselves but in the music as a complete package. Unlike many genres of music which adapt their lyrics to fit the English language to appeal to a wider market – makers of Black Metal do not consider this to be an important selling point. The sale and distribution of Black Metal is handled differently to most other genres. Roger Tiegs (aka 'Infernus' guitarist of *Gorgoroth*) has said in interview that 'one shouldn't have to support a Black Metal band' (Moynihan & Søderlind, 2003: 326). Indicating that rarely did such artists see their music as a consumable product and they reject the capitalist marketing strategies mainly used to sell music to the masses. Through their status as relatively unmarketable, the musicians of extreme metal scenes have embraced this and are prepared to take risks that artists who are solely career musicians cannot. More than this – the use of languages possibly alien to the listener performs multiple roles. Primarily, the musicians sing in a language that is most familiar to them and they will not fall foul of translation mistakes. By singing in this language, they are igniting the spirit of their culture in the listener, and simultaneously creating a boundary of exclusivity within the subculture that suggests that foreign fans have to work, to translate it, to be an active part of the fan base.

Rebelling against modernity by referring to the Norse mythos is more than a representation of religious separatism. The Old Norse mythologies are as culturally significant as they are spiritually. By the same logic, the Greek gods of Olympus are much-loved aspects of Greek culture, although worshipping them is no longer an issue. By continuing to weave the ancient stories into their music, they are honouring the past and displaying a disdain for the weak, pitiful world as they see it now. Once again, we can interlink with the sovereign wolf. Embodied by the ancient world and embittered by the current world. The Black Metal subculture members and associates are commonly found to adorn themselves in pendants of 'Mjolnir', Thor's mythical hammer, which was originally worn by Viking warriors to ward off bad luck at sea. Whether the belief in the symbol as a luck charm is relevant or not, the aspect of this ritual that should be adhered to is its presence. The wearing of the symbol itself is a conscious acceptance of one's culture. It is the removal of the symbol of Mjolnir from a construct of religion to culture that places it on a different level to Christians who wear a cross necklace. The intrinsic connection between the individual Norwegian and the symbol, Mjolnir, exerts the relationship of national cultural ownership of the relic in a way entirely different to the relationship between the English and the Crucifix. The Crucifix is an overtly religious symbol and denotes the belief structure of the wearer, displaying a sense of allegiance to the faith.

If one reads the Poetic Edda or the libraries of books appertaining to the Old Norse Gods attributed to, amongst others, Snorri Sturulson, one will notice that even a direct translation is not entirely helpful in understanding the narrative. This is due to the differences in story-telling style between cultures. Below is the opening stanza of the Norse poem 'Voluspa' in three forms. The first being as it was collected it in the Poetic Edda. The second, a direct translation of the passage from Old Icelandic to English and the third the translation transposed into the narrative style that we understand today.

> 1. 'Hljóðs bið ek allar
>   helgar kindir,
>   meiri ok minni
>   mögu Heimdallar;
>   viltu, at ek, Valföðr!
>   vel framtelja
>   forn spjöll fíra,
>   þau er fremst um man'.

> 2. 'I ask for silence from them all
>   Sacred families,
>   Large or small
>   Sons of the world tree;
>   You will, that I, father of the chosen.
>   Tell well
>   The old stories
>   To those who are the first among men'.

Here, the skald (poet) is asking for silence from everyone (the children of World Tree), as the assembled audience is well aware that the skald is by far the best at telling the stories of the old gods to the winners of the 'bride's races' an early Nordic custom (Vikernes, 2011).

With the second version, a direct translation brings the opening speech into the realm of the medieval dramatic, but still lacks the narrative style that would make it tenable to western sensibilities. The third version is the clearest as the explanation is given as to who is speaking to whom, and what they are requesting. This ancient style of Nordic story-telling spread across the world, and as detail regarding dress, style, the landscape, etc. is sparse to non-existent the story could be recalled through speech from memory quite easily with the imaginations of the listeners filling in the gaps. It is interesting to note that Vikernes comments that primitive man possessed a higher intelligence, an argument supported by the recent hypothesis of geneticist Crabtree (2012), thus never needing to write things down or produce works of art as ancient society never repressed the wolf in man. However, this position has drawn much debate in itself as to its veracity (Mitchell, 2012). Interlinking with the two previous themes, he claims the cave paintings proof that primitive man needed only pictures to exemplify a situation perfectly. If taken to be true, with this style of story-telling the receptiveness of the audience is clearly as significant to the success of the skald, as their recall ability itself. Some Norwegian Black Metal bands in Norway embrace this style of story-telling in their lyrics, consider the lyrics for '[Black] Spell of Destruction' by *Burzum* (below). This is a further adoption of ancient Scandinavian culture to the Black Metal subculture. Writing lyrics in this skaldic technique, as opposed to the more common narrative style, reject modernity, and align themselves with the Norway of Old.

> Hear my Sword
> ...in the Making
> Of my Spell
> Literally
> Damkuna, Iftraga
> Sheb Nigurepur, Dafast
> The World's Tragedy, Is Served at My Feast.

Atavism in Norway: A reaction against government and policy

Norway has a socio-democratic Governmental system. A system that supports the use of social intervention and welfare to enable social justice within a capitalist framework. Heywood (2012: 128) defines social democracy as:

> [A]n ideological stance that supports a broad balance between market capitalism, on the one hand, and state intervention, on the other hand. Being based on a compromise between the market and the state, social democracy lacks a systematic underlying theory and is, arguably, inherently vague. It is nevertheless associated with the following views: (1) capitalism is the only reliable means of generating wealth, but it is a morally defective means of distributing wealth because of its tendency towards poverty and inequality; (2) the defects of the capitalist system can be rectified through economic and social intervention, the state being the custodian of the public interest...

In the 1990's, the era that the Black Metal subculture formed, the Norwegian Labour Party was in sole possession of the Government. The history of Norwegian governance, particularly during World War II has led to a system in which any right-wing party is marginalised and prevented from holding power (Bangstad, 2015). This has recently shifted, and a new populist right is gaining ground, riding on the back of amongst other things, the current refugee crisis (ibid.). During the Second World War, the then-Prime Minister Vidkun Quisling (Dahl, 1999: 215), collaborated with the Nazis in the occupation of Norway and effectively sold out his country (Dahl, 1999: 219–225). His actions earned the perpetrator's name to be synonymous with 'traitor'. Following the conclusion of the conflict he was executed to mass public approval. The treachery performed by Quisling has led to a situation of an innate fear in the activities of the right-wing. This has repeated through-out Europe (Bangstad, 2015). Such parties are monitored closely or forcefully disbanded in case of any possible repeat. The results have been mixed at best. Positively the polity has remained rigid with a series of policies that can be comfortably continued through successive cabinets. Of course, as well as being an agreeable system for all parties to allow agreeable policies to flour-ish, it also means that potentially unpleasant ones with negative consequences for the electorate will remain in the policy book. On the other hand, the right wing has been forced underground where their activities cannot be moni-tored, so although they do not have a legitimate voice to skew Governance, in retaliation-tragedies that took place like those on Utoya Island, committed by Anders Breivik in the summer of 2011 were made more likely.

The integration of church and state in Norway has developed into the two being seen as one agency. Consequently, the churches become a symbol of the Government's intrusion. Any protest against the Church is likely to be as equally scathing on the Government too. The atavistic nature of the attacks on the churches in the 1990's can be interpreted as the arsonists using man-kind's oldest and most feared weapon on both Christianity and Government. The wooden stave churches burned in symbolic blazes of disquiet, and although the Government treated the incidents as connected arson attacks by Satanists, it is undoubtedly the apolitical nature of the event hid an overtly political protest, due to the intrinsic links between church and state.

As a socio-democratic nation, any rebellion against the state is more likely to be that of the sovereign wolf, an act of an individual. Looking back at the idea of the sovereign, we can see that the wolf believes him-self to be above the law and rejects the protection and subjugation that the state requires (Hoffin, 2019). If we look at this in the context of the kill-ings on Utoya Island by Anders Breivik; this attack was condemned by all the right-wing parties that previously would have quite happily made the same political dialogue beforehand. Thus, there is a right-wing contingency driven dangerously underground and therefore off the radar and a lone wolf preying on innocents. Breivik ascertained that he was 'sending a message' about the upcoming Islamification of Europe, and specifically Norway. He proceeded to achieve this by murdering youth members of the Governing Party, Labour. Many commentators balked at the killing of white teenagers in an attack that claimed to be about an incoming Islamic threat. If we can consider this from the ideology of the sovereign and the atavist, by reject-ing the laws of the state and the protection it offers, Breivik had effectively become the wolf, alien to his countrymen. Making his attacks more relevant to his message than a strike on the Islamic faithful. By using the violence to appropriate his message, he can be described as profoundly atavist.

Atavism in Norway can also be looked at in terms of anti-globalisation. Norway possesses a population with a notably xenophobic streak (Taylor, 2010). Norway has voted against entry into the European Union (EU), and only signed the Schengen Agreement in 1996, implementing it in 2001. As Gro Harlem Brundtland's Labour Government lifted an Act during her Cabinet in the 1990's which amounted to an almost complete ban on immigration. Originally imposed in 1975, it only allowed access for family members, students, experts, and refugees/asylum seekers. Now all migrants to Norway are required to undertake 250 hours in tuition on the national language. This is still a relaxed attitude compared to prior Governments. The influx of immigration that this relaxation allowed produced an accelerated globalising effect on a country that held and still holds an incredibly Caucasian majority.

Nazism as performative politics

The Black Metal subculture's Nazism has long been thought of as a culmination of the far-right among youth in Norway. This chapter posits that the situation is more complex. The central figures of the Black Metal 'inner circle' were adamant that they wished to present themselves as a force of evil (Aites & Ewell, 2009). In direct contrast to the parallel extreme metal subgenre of 'Death Metal', which Aarseth among others would call 'Life Metal' due to the scene's chosen aesthetics and forays into 'positive' politics (Sanchez, 2005), although secretly, Euronymous was in close contact, tape-trading with the likes of Shane Embury of UK Death Metal/grindcore band, Napalm Death (Moynihan & Søderlind, 2003). When encouraged to consider their presentation, a few chose to adopt traits of Nazism, for performative purposes. Their main focus was to appear evil and/or Satanic. Jonas Akerlund (director of 'Lords of Chaos' and ex-drummer with *Bathory*) sees the descent into a performative Nazism: 'I don't think they had a political agenda. I know that some of them are very extreme in their political agenda today, but they were young boys'. (Godfrey, 2019). He indicates that the macabre one-upmanship that typified the Second Wave of Black Metal (resulting in suicide, arson, and murder), was the result of immaturity where 'they stopped thinking as individuals and started thinking more as a group, to impress each other, and to shock' (ibid.) The subculture allowed itself to become an echo chamber, forming its own entity, apart from societal rules, where the only thing that mattered would be being seen as more extreme than everyone else and therefore attaining valuable subcultural capital (Thornton, 1995; Huq, 2006). As the liminal space for such transgressive extremity is created, Akerlund claims that the subjects become 'immune' where they could 'take one step further, and then another, and before [they] know it, it's not a big deal to kill a man' (ibid.). Erik Danielsson of Swedish Black Metal band *Watain* shares this conclusion, stating that: '[Performing Black Metal] hardens you and it gets you to the point where you just do not give a f***' (Doran, 2012). The further the groups enveloped themselves in their subcultural abyss, the shorter the leaps became between atrocities, with Nazism one of the many extremities that became enshrined through the nature of its cumulative harm (and perception of harms) in order to shock and appal the sensibilities, in a manner comparable to early New York and London punk scenes, where musicians would adopt Nazi iconography to subvert the attitudes of parents; some of whom were Jewish and had lived under the Nazi regime (O'Hara, 1999).

As the scene evolved, artists who were drawn to actual Nazism would align to the subculture and creating music that would eventually become known as NSBM (National Socialist Black Metal). As the space for such milieu had already been put in place, artists like Varg Vikernes of Burzum, who had previously been a part of the far-right 'skinhead' scene in Norway throughout the 1980s, became prolific Black Metal figures (Goodricke-Clarke, 2002). Although it is debatable to the extent that even early Burzum would promote Vikernes' racist views lyrically (Baddeley, 2010). His 'signature' song (i.e., the song he feels best promotes the band's message) 'Feeble Screams from Forests Unknown' (Deathlike Silence Productions, 1992) (lyrics below) reads as a doctrine of how humanity is weaker, more feeble, and more unable to understand the arcane knowledge that led early man to hunt, build civilisations, and dominate.

> Drifting
> In the air
> Above a cold lake
> Is a soul
> From an early
> Better age
> Grasping for
> A mystic thought
> In vain ... but who's to know
> Further on lies eternal search
> For theories to lift the gate
> Only locks are made stronger
> And more keys lost as logic fades
> In the pool of dreams the water darkens
> For the soul that's tired of search
> As years pass by
> The aura drops
> As less and less
> Feelings touch
> Stupidity
> Has won too much
> The hopeless soul
> Keeps mating[1]

A subculture of atavism, recalling politics of atavism

As mentioned above, a feature that defines Second Wave Black Metal is its collective disdain for modernity and reverence for primitivist methods. This message carries through both lyrics and lo-fidelity musical construction of the sonic landscape itself (Hoffin, 2018). This statement of intent engenders itself to political doctrines that also hold the 'old ways' in high regard. Nazism contains multitudes of symbols that hark back to the Pagan roots that Norwegian Black Metal artists draw such a distinct connection to. The promises made by Nazi ideology were also of particular interest to the BM community, with focus on the power of the strong over the weak, the destruction of Judeo-Christian religions, and the will to power and the Scandinavian phenomenon of 'likhet' (the state of visual similarity between people, i.e. race (Gullestad, 2004) which translated very easily on to the racist attitudes of Nazism. Both Nazism and Black Metal found themselves in each other's proximity via their shared appreciation for the teachings and tropes of Paganism, it is from this lens that this section will elucidate the connections.

The runes that make up the Elder Furthark (second—eighth century) (Page, 2005), share both aesthetic and meaning with numerous icons found through Nazi iconography. The 'S' of the logo of Hitler's secret Police, is derived from the Pagan 'sowlio', which translates as 'sun', Himmler's occult specialist Karl Maria Willgut further translated this symbol to become 'sig', becoming a symbol representing 'victory' (Hale, 2003). 'Algiz', another symbol, ('z') came to represent the resistance to sacrificing heritage (Page, 1999). These two symbols alone present a commonality between Nazism and the Norwegian's Black Metal culture. However, these concepts should be understood as orbiting the proximity of each other. Problematically, this creates the space and a perfect breeding ground that the far-right can exploit and gain entry into the Subculture. As there is very little necessity for subversion of culturally-accepted tropes and symbols, and a nudge into far-right politics of a scene that existed within a wider culture that promotes visual likeness as an ideal.

Second Wave Black Metal espouses a return to Pagan values with a determination to purge Christianity and Christian symbols from Norway. Vikernes once commented on the rationale behind the numerous church burnings throughout Scandinavia, declaring the lack of respect that Christians had building churches on 'Pagan holy ground' justifies the arson (Aites & Ewell, 2009).

Cascadian Black Metal or blackening the green and greening the black

The atavistic spirit of Black Metal has, in certain scenes, diverged from the 'evil' nature; creating a subgenre that openly reveres the natural world, adding an ecological perspective while keeping a similar sonic template. Long-flowing passages, evoking the chaotic rhythms of the nature, the subtle violence inherent in the natural world. Eschewing the call for the decay of human civilisation, as previous Black Metal art would align to, the 'Cascadian' scene, which it came to be known as, after the geographical area of its naissance, negates modern human civilisation by ignoring it completely (Hoffin, 2018). Wilson's coining of the term 'melancology', provides a qualifier for Black Metal as a twisted form of ecologically conscious writing, where the natural world becomes an unstoppable oppressive force (Wilson, 2014). As a result, we can observe and analyse Black Metal outside of 'human' civilisation as an extension to and critique of political behaviours (Hatemi & McDermott, 2011). By presenting nature as profoundly negative that 'blackens the cosmos' (Wilson, 2014), Black Metal itself becomes reframed as a hostile body pushing back against the normalised material civilisation. As Black Metal must retain its oppositional and 'evil' stance to be Black Metal, casting flora and fauna as pseudo-antagonists or powerful, destructive forces in an eternal, esoteric struggle seems quite appropriate. Consequently, opening a space for more consciously left-leaning thought, forging its way into the blackened spotlight. The Cascadian Black Metal movement helped to partially unhinge Black Metal from its perceived right-wing slant while maintaining its core anti-modernity tenet but allowed the scene to diversify its membership and once again, open up an epistemological space for new voices and ideas that could be expressed sonically, lyrically, or through performance.

Conclusion and the contemporary far-right in Black Metal

In prolonged campaigns by concerned musicians and interested groups, a number of bands/artists who possess political views of the extreme right variety or are associated with/members of white supremacist groups have been exposed. The sheer number of racist, sexist, and/or queerphobic members near the top of the subcultural hierarchy is shocking but not really a surprise to those who find themselves uncomfortably immersed in the subculture, as many of these artists felt free to express themselves anyway; these far-right sympathies were hardly kept secret. The Norwegian Duo of *Fenriz* and *Nocturno Culto* who make up *Darkthrone*, despite claiming their distance from politics, explained away the phrase 'Norsk Arisk Black Metal' (Norwegian Aryan Black Metal) appearing on the reverse of early copies of *Transilvanian Hunger* with the possibly even worse statement: 'We would like to state that Transilvanian Hunger stands beyond any criticism. If any man should attempt to criticize this LP, he should be thoroughly patronized for his obviously Jewish behavio[u]r' (Wiederhorn, 2014). They apologised and stated that 'Arisk' was meant to mean 'true' (a popular epithet attached to the scene) or 'pure', that 'Jewish', in Norwegian was a slang term, meaning 'something that is out of order', and that they could have written 'stupid' instead (ibid.). This could be read as one example of musicians who had been given the benefit of the doubt one too many times. However, since this early controversy, it has been very difficult to find any further evidence of Nazism within *Darkthrone's* enduring career. Two possibilities for this can be theorised; first, that the band really did not mean to come off as racists and that their wording became problematic once introduced to an international market or that the inherent shock value in making the statement was their principal goal. Being admonished and removed from the Peaceville label that was putting out Darkthrone's records was enough to make them question their actions and apologise. Of course, there is a possibility that Darkthrone were indeed proscribed to Nazism, but the lack of any further forays into fascism makes that unlikely.

Note

1 Burzum, (1992), "Feeble Screams from Forests Unknown", *Burzum* [CD], Oslo, Norway: Deathlike Silence Productions.

References

Aites, A. and Ewell, A., (2009), *Until the Light Takes Us* [Documentary], New York: Variance Films.

Baddeley, G., (2010), *Lucifer Rising: A Book of Sin, Devil Worship and Rock n' Roll*, 3rd edition, London: Plexus Publishing Ltd.

Bangstad, S., (2015), "The Rise of the Populist Right in Norway", *Boston Review* [online], Available at: http://bostonreview.net/world/sindre-bangstad-norway-populist-right [Last Accessed 9 March 2022].

Beste, P., (2008), *True Norwegian Black Metal*, London: VICE.

Burzum, (1992), "Feeble Screams from Forests Unknown", *Burzum* [CD], Oslo, Norway: Deathlike Silence Productions.

Campbell, G., et al., (1994), *Cultural Atlas of the Viking Age*, Birmingham: Andromeda.

Crabtree, G.R., (2012), "Our Fragile Intellect. Part I". *Trends in Genetics*, 29(1), pp. 1–3.

Dahl, H.F., (1999), *Quisling: A Study in Treachery*, Cambridge: Cambridge University Press.

Doran, J., (2012), "Sympathy for the Devil", *Metal Hammer*, 234, pp. 41–45, London: Future Publishing.

Dubois, T.A., (1999), *Nordic Religions in the Viking Age*, Philadelphia: University of Pennsylvania Press.

Darkthrone, (1992), *A Blaze in the Northern Sky* [CD], London, UK: Peaceville Productions.

Darkthrone, (1993), *Under a Funeral Moon* [CD], London, UK: Peaceville Productions.

Darkthrone, (1994), *Transilvanian Hunger* [CD], London, UK: Peaceville Productions.

Emperor, (1994), *In The Nightside Eclipse* [CD], Helsinki, Finland: Candlelight Records.

Godfrey, A., (2019), 'Before you know it, it's not a big deal to kill a man': Norwegian black metal's murderous past. *The Guardian*, 22 March, Available at: https://www.theguardian.com/music/2019/mar/22/before-you-know-it-its-not-a-big-deal-to-kill-a-man-norwegian-black-metals-murderous-past [Last Accessed 10 March 2022].

Goodricke-Clarke, N., (2002), *Black Sun: Aryan Cults, Esoteric Nazism and the Politics of Identity*, New York: New York University Press.

Gullestad, M., (2004), "Blind Slaves of our Prejudices: Debating 'Culture' and 'Race' in Norway", *Ethnos: Journal of Anthropology*, 69(2), pp. 177–203.

Hale, C., (2003), *Himmler's Crusade: The Nazi Expedition to Find the Origins of the Aryan Race*, Hoboken: John Wiley & Sons.

Hatemi, P.K. and McDermott, R., (eds.), (2011), *Man Is by Nature a Political Animal: Evolution, Biology, and Politics*, Chicago: Chicago University Press.

Heywood, A., (2012), *Political Ideologies: An Introduction*, 5th edition, Basingstoke: Palgrave MacMillan.

Hoffin, K., (2018), "Decay as a Black Metal Symbol", *Metal Music Studies*, 4(1), pp. 81–94, doi: 10.1386/mms.4.1.81_1

Hoffin, K., (2019), "'Sans Compassion nor Will to Answer Whoever Asketh the Why': Personal Sovereignty within Black Metal", *Metal Music Studies*, 5(2), pp. 151–162. doi: 10.1386/mms.5.2.151_1

Hoffin, K., (2020), "Glocalization, Bricolage and Black Metal: Towards a Music-Centric Youth Culture Simultaneously Exemplifying the Global and the Glocal", *Metal Music Studies*, 6(1), pp. 27–48, doi: 10.1386/mms_00003_1

Howells, T., (ed.), (2012), *Black Metal: Beyond the Darkness*, London: Black Dog Publishing.

Huq, R., (2006), *Beyond Subculture: Pop, Youth and Identity in a Postcolonial World*, Oxford: Routledge.

Kahn-Harris, K., (2003), "The Aesthetics of Hate Music", Institute of Jewish Policy Research [online], Available at: https://archive.jpr.org.uk/download?id=2235 [Last Accessed 9 March 2022].

Kahn-Harris, K., (2007), *Extreme Metal: Music and Culture on the Edge*, London: Berg.

Mayhem, (1994), *De Mysteriis Dom Sathanas* [CD] Oslo, Norway: Deathlike Silence Productions.

Mitchell, K.J., (2012), "Genetic Entropy and the Human Intellect", *Trends in Genetics*, 29 (2), pp. 59–60.

Moynihan, M. and Søderlind, D., (2003), *Lords of Chaos: The Bloody Rise of The Satanic Metal Underground*, 2nd edition, Washington: Feral House.

Nordeide, W.S., (2007), *The Christianisation of Norway*, Bergen: Centre for Medieval Studies, University of Bergen.

O'Hara, C., (1999), *The Philosophy of Punk: More than Noise*, Edinburgh: AK Press.

Page, R.I., (1999), *An Introduction to English Runes*, Woodridge: Boydell Press.

Page, R.I., (2005), *Runes*, London: The British Museum Press.

Patterson, D., (2013), *Black Metal: Evolution of the Cult*, Washington: Feral House.

Sanchez, R.C., (2005), "Dead & Buried: Mayhem" *Terrorizer Magazine: Black Metal Special #128*, London: Dark Arts Ltd.

Savage, J., (2005), *England's Dreaming: Sex Pistols and Punk Rock*, London: Faber and Faber.

Taylor, L.W., (2010), "Nordic Nationalisms: Black Metal Takes Norway's Everyday Racism to the Extreme", *The Metal Void: The First Gatherings*, Oxford: Inter-Disciplinary Press.

Thornton, S., (1995), *Club Cultures: Music, Media, and Subcultural Capital.* Cambridge: Polity Press.

Vikernes, V., (2004), "The Viking Age and Christianity in Norway", *Burzum.org* [online], Available at: http://www.burzum.org/eng/library/the_viking_age_and_ christianity_in_norway.shtml [Last Accessed 9 March 2022].

Vikernes, V., (2011), "4.2 Freyr's First Group of Eight", *Sorcery and Religion in Ancient Scandinavia*, London: Abstract Sounds Ltd.

Wiederhorn, J., (2014), "Happy 20th Birthday to Darkthrone's Controversial Black Metal Masterpiece, Transilvanian Hunger", *Vice* [online], Available at: https:// www.vice.com/en/article/r7qdyr/happy-20th-birthday-to-darkthrones-controver-sial-black-metal-masterpiece-transilvanian-hunger [Last Accessed 9 March 2022].

Wilson, S., (ed.), (2014), *Melancology: Black Metal Theory and Ecology*, Alresford: Zero Books.

Wittman, P., (1910), *'Haakon the Good,' The Catholic Encyclopaedia*, New York: Robert Appleton Company [online]. Available at: http://www.newadvent.org/ cathen/07116b.htm [Last Accessed 10 March 2022].

4 Musical Experience as Penumbra, Haecceity, and Utopian Fractal

Musica Penumbra

Craig Hammond

Roland Barthes in his essay *Musica Practica* posits that there are two types of music, 'the music one listens to, [and] the music one plays' (Barthes, 1977a, p. 149). According to this basic schema of musical experience, the Barthesean category of *listening* refers to – and belies – an unpredictable realm of unique and creative practice. Here, personal and personalised encounters with audible culture resonate as interior activities, mimetic impulses that *spin out* as interpretive escapes (Barthes, 1977a, p. 152). Such moments of associative freedom audibly refract the experience of musical listening, shifting it from a scenario where a recipient passively absorbs an external and stable segment of sound, to one where they intuitively engage with it as a *composer-in-collaboration*, and respond to associative provocations that splinter from the audible source. In this way, the repercussive experience of listening involves the revelation of something *inaudible*, the extra rhythmic and unpredictable transmission of a surplus meaning. Rather than implanting the linear reception of a static performance, active musical listening prompts a process of recomposition, where an active witness sifts the sonoric debris for buds of new and malleable meaning. Each expressionistic witness engages with the shifting impact of reverberating impulses and rhythms, that infiltrate and agitate as an array of fermentations (Cseres, 2017, p. 151). In this way listening is connected to the productive and constitutive principles of hermeneutics – a glossolalic attitude of revelation and heuristic decoding (Barthes, 1991, p. 249). Hence, to actively listen to music is to treat it as an audio palimpsest, and to *affectively* infuse it with a fresh inscription.

For Jeongwon & Song (2002) the reconstructive act of musical listening is therefore an unruly and random encounter – where a participative witness expressionistically engages with sound traces to produce a destabilised *text* of meaning. The Barthesean notion of *text* in relation to music is important here, as its etymology is *texere* (which means 'to weave'), and *texo* (which means 'I weave'). Therefore, expositional ruminations on audible culture become nomadic, iterative, and autonomic – they open up an experience that replaces the presence, legacy, and coherence of the original composer. This sonoric *death of the author* means that the transmission and reception of

DOI: 10.4324/9781003186410-4

music becomes a *fertile* process, where transversal echoes oscillate between the source and the receiver in an open space of parallax and fracture.[1] In the authorial lacuna, the interiority of the liberating listener weaves and *folds* an ontological fabric of subversive and transformative potential.

In this way the Barthesean approach to the experience of musical listening establishes a distinction between its reception as a completed piece of culture 'work', and – in opposition to this – an incomplete and flexible encounter, as part of the ongoing production of a culture infused 'text' (Barthes, 1978, p. 6). In this sense the subjective experience of music does not perpetuate a trammelled and predictable response or an intact preservation of an unimpinged and unchanging piece of culture. Instead, by piquing the quicksilver terrain of a collaborator's interiority, sonoric traces become dithyrambic smudges, charged with metamorphosed inversions and textual fecundities (Barthes, 1991, p. 248; Jeongwon & Song, 2002, p. 267).

Of course, musical artefacts – produced and disseminated on the *outside* – remain as external sources, as distantiated, segmented, and repeated pieces of culture work. However, when internalised and experienced as a subliminal and undulating text, they become imbued with the bespoken and fluid tenets of language. Importantly for Barthes, such subterfugal listening encounters do not decompose the integrity of the external piece of music; but rather recognise it as a range of phantasmagoric vectors emanating as a flotsam from the 'imaginary tail' of the source (Barthes, 1977b, p. 157). Experienced as a textual fission, musical listening initiates a dilatory serial of internal 'movements, disonnections, overlappings, and variations' (Barthes, 1977b, p. 158); heterogeneities of perspective that facilitate an ambiguity and *plurality* of reference points and echoes. Ruptured from its external platform, this notion of *musical-experience-as-internal-text* suggests an intricate weave of 'obscure, blurred, or otherwise mute' associations (Barthes, 1991, p. 249), made up of a memory-pocked web, inlaid with sparks and shards of unique perspective.

In a related sense, Cseres (2017) notes that for Giles Deleuze and Félix Guattari, the strange correspondence between world, music, and individuality is not something that unravels as part of a mechanical or mathematically stable formulae. Quite the inverse, it uncovers a chaotic and unstable cartography (p. 152). For Deleuze in particular, once imbibed, the singularity of a musical trace becomes embedded as a dormant and gestative *fold* (Deleuze, 2006b, p. 156).[2] In this sense we can refer to the expressionistic and infused incursion of a *sonoric fold*, as something where the matrices of memory become spliced with refracted music-text splinters that develop as a 'relation to oneself, or the affect on self by self' (Deleuze, 2006c, p. 107). In this sense, a sonoric fold can be defined as 'an allegorical chamber of instantiated music-tinged memory'; a metaphorical thought vessel; an illuviated fold of introspective and unique ingredients hued with experience and association (Deleuze, 2006b, p. 24).

The *outside* realm of – what we can now term as – *music-as-culture-work*, is emitted across a complex horizon. An exterior space of chaotic waves and intersecting multi-flows that accumulate as non-linear entanglements that contain the potential for sonoric intensities. As a smorgasbord of musical projections, they wash unpredictably against the visceral surface of the body. From this, sonoric folds submerge as accumulated textual deposits, which somnambulate beneath the subjective lamina of *Being*. Through time and experience this proto-creative dust of music-infused happenstances develop into improvisational texts – a *leavening* 'stuff' of dynamic and shifting thought matter (Deleuze, 2006c, pp. 120–121). As sublimated and lixiviated strata, musical encounters thus scatter throughout the personalised terrain of everyday life, and as sonoric folds they accumulate and harbor as ciphered bundles of difference, mutable dormancies, and seeds of transformation (Deleuze, 2006c, p. 116).

As reverberations of requiem, sonoric folds oscillate between the dormant repose of somnambulism and purposeful acts of future Becoming. They refibrillate from dormancy through the *sporadic random functions* of association and memorial chance (Mandelbrot, 1999, p. 248), and murmur in non-linear and unpredictable ways as hermetic hieroglyphs. Considered in conjunction with the Barthesean notion of musical listening, sonoric folds thus embed as itinerant granules that encompass the plurality of 'free, wild or untamed differences' (Deleuze, 2001, p. 50). Memorial refibrillation means that sonoric folds conglomerate and striate to produce emergent irruptions of new meaning; conferring expressive and unpredictable detours on to the corporeality of subjective matter, and facilitate new stories in the form of *texts-of-possibility* (Deleuze, 2006b, p. 39). In sum, the mosaic of Barthesean and Deleuzean concepts encompassing musical listening, the elicitative text, and sonoric folding present instances of musical experience that permutate as undulating and kaleidoscopic shifts. They direct us towards – and uncover – an objectively inaccessible interiority, to reveal a deeply subjective interior shadow of creative musical experiences that manifest and mutate as a reverberative and kinetic weave. Cumulatively, these folded and refracted music infusions bundle to form a collective paene of memorial umbra's; spliced with cherished and improvisational tunes, dissected lyrics, and other transmorphic sonoric traces.

To conceptually encapsulate this complex and multifaceted process I wish to develop and apply the term *musica penumbra*. The word penumbra derives from the Latin terms *paene* and *umbra*; when combined, these literally mean 'almost shadow'. In astronomical terms, the word refers to a particular stage within the process of a lunar eclipse, specifically the 'space between the shadow cast by the earth and the complete illumination from the sun' (Gingerich, 2008, p. 569). Coined by Johannes Kepler in 1604, a *penumbra* emerges on the 'side of the moon which is just about to have a taste of shadow' (Kepler, 2000, p. 252). However, our take on the penumbra here, is of course an ontologised variation, adapted to conceptualise and iterate the subjective, reflexive, and interior spaces that form as a result of dialogic musical encounters (Merz & Merz, 2017, p. 2). The ontologised notion of *musica penumbra*, here, is therefore intended to act as a kind of cryptograph, a revelatory cipher to refer to and loosely articulate the interior sheaving of musical folds. As a complex dust, *musica penumbra* deluminates the external world and casts an inner light on to the ambiguity of self-referential clusters of music-text shadows (Blumenberg, 1993, p. 34). In this sense, the closing of the eyes, in the meditatory pursuit of an audible *line of flight*, suggests a metaphorical eclipse; a transcendence beyond the outside and into a shadow world of interiority; an incursive expedition towards accumulated folds and recessed cusps of potent thought-matter. As a collection of introversive slips, music-hued penumbral shadows murmur with audible traces that morph into a cryptic legion of possibilities.

As an array of mereological splinters, a musica penumbra is an agglomeration of sonor-inspired thought assemblage; a billowing form of deterritorialised music ruptures that have broken away from external chains of meaning and signification (Deleuze & Guattari, 1986, pp. 5–6). Forming as an illuvial fan of auditory hieroglyphs, the penumbra, cleft by memory-spliced encounters, ruminates in the heuristic sanctums, and existential interiors of our crypts. In a Deleuzean sense, the memorial refibrillation of a penumbra prompts accumulated sonoric folds to flutter with unique subvocalisations of 'minority' texts in the form of a *minority gesture* (Deleuze, 2006a, p. 159).[3] Through a cryptic and idiomatic language of minority possibility, emergent Becoming takes flight in creative and subjectively meaningful ways. This minority language of a musical gesture (a *penumbral refrain* within Deleuzoguattarian parlance) is infused with stutters of sonoric memory, which in turn prompts the imagination to murmur with subjective-hued and future-potent aspirations (Deleuze, 1997, p. 110).[4] As a separate and distinct soundscape, the minority gesture that emerges from the penumbral refrain is important within a Deleuzoguattarian framework, as they note, 'we call a refrain any aggregate of matters of expression that draws a territory and develops into territorial motifs', a sonorous assemblage that is 'dominated' by sound and memory (Deleuze & Guattari, 2005, p. 323). A penumbral refrain therefore internally manifests as a mutative minority text, an internal harbinger of transformation, personal hope, and possibility.

Musica penumbra and haecceity

As such, *musica penumbra* as an accumulation of sonoric folds evolves as further incursive incidents occur, (incursion here is related to the Latin terms *incurro* and *incurrere*, which mean to 'run in to' or 'invade'). As a bundled accumulation of sonoric folds the *musica penumbra* and its associated gestural refrains become active and emanate as an excursive text (excursion here is related to the Latin terms *excurro* and *excurrere*, which refer 'to running outwards' or 'projecting'). As such the initial incursive act of musical listening prompts the hermeneutic ingestion of an aural trace which deposits as a fold; this subsequently sheaves and stutters into a coalescent music-hued refrain (Duffy, 2017, p. 191). From a bundled assemblage the penumbral refrain striates, loops, and knots as a gestative 'line of drift', budding and billowing along eccentric movements and gestures (Deleuze & Guattari, 2005, pp. 311–312). In this sense, the minority nature of a penumbral refrain erupts from the shadow as an emanative, excursive, and improvised thought pattern. Provoked out of dormancy, the refrain as a disjunctive act mutates beyond the contours of memory as a random variable (Mandelbrot, 1999, p. 261). As a minority utterance this subvocal voice from the shadow of the interior emerges as a chaotic occurrence; it is a unique and interior text that morphs beyond pre-existing thoughts, to reveal the unconscious potential of everyday life (Duffy, 2017, p. 197).

Importantly, for Deleuze and Guattari complex and fundamental modes of memory-based individuation (termed here as a *penumbral refrain*), occurs within – and across – each and every human being. However, whilst such occurrences are shared and experienced as a trans-human essence, each intra-subjective manifestation shifts along irrevocable dissimilarities from person to person. Deleuze and Guattari attribute the term *haecceity* to this strange and non-linear facet of individuation (Deleuze & Guattari, 2003, p. 261). Originally coined by the medieval scholastic philosopher John Duns Scotus (1266–1308), haecceity refers to the subjective and unique properties of individuated identity. As such, haecceity as a concept refers to the incomparable *something* that populates the interiority and identity of each separate person (Scotus, 1963, pp. 166–167). Adapted from the Latin term *haec*, which means 'this', haecceity articulates the specificity of subjective and personalised 'thisness'. It is often counterposed against the term quiddity, which is taken from the Latin term *quid*, meaning 'what'; and tends to be equated with the more quintessential and generalised notion of 'whatness'. Where quiddity refers to the inter-human sharing of a common nature or other existential phenomenon, haecceity refers to the fractured and internal substance of difference; a subliminal or penumbral ether that makes each and every one of us unique (Bates, 2010, p. 91). Ultimately, as a pocket of individual difference, a haecceity is an idiosyncratic portion of unique perspective, a self-divided fraction, or abstracted part from within the individual apparatus of Being. As a conceptual reference for individuality, haecceity denotes the human experience of specific folding in relation to time and place, 'the folding of becoming' (Wortel, 2011, p. 2). Or, as Rosenkrantz defines, 'any concrete entity, *a*, has a haecceity, an irreducibly nonqualitative property or "thisness" of being identical with a' (Rosenkrantz, 1993, p. xiii).

Importantly, haecceity should *not* be considered as a simple piece of existential décor or a superficial backdrop to the core of subjective identity. Rather it should be understood as an ontologic fabric – or text – of internal and woven assemblages, that combine to form the aggregated make-up of each conscious individual. Ultimately, 'we' are haecceity, (or rather, our selfhood consists of an accumulation of haecceities) which, when combined, give form to the incomparable uniqueness of self (Deleuze & Guattari, 2003, p. 262). Haecceity can therefore be used here as a contributory conceptual offering for the ways in which we engage with and internally orient ourselves to music. For example, within the conceptual schema developed so far, the *quiddity* of music refers to the general circulation of pre-established and completed culture-works across external terrains. As quiddity, this generic notion of music distribution encapsulates the production and dissemination of audible culture as a packaged and stable medium. Thus, the quiddity of music can be used to refer to the socio-cultural dispensing of genre, ideology, and other sonoric messages of style and fashion. However, subjected to the parameters of haecceity, musical listening and experience equates to its internal malleation as a flexible text. Aligned with the incursive qualities of sonoric folding and the shifting essence of the penumbral refrain, music as haecceity inhabits each of our interior worlds in odd and relativistic ways. As an abstracted manifestation, a music-infused refrain is haecceic in that it discerns the existential experience of music as a subjective turbulence. As such, a penumbral refrain does not simply *emplace* the external replication of a piece of music, but rather, transforms as a haecceity through an accumulation of folds into a facet of minority individuation (Deleuze & Guattari, 2003, p. 261).

Music as haecceity therefore emerges as a *nomadic essence*, a vague yet rigorous *continuum* of variation that connects to – and with – the metamorphosis of being (Deleuze & Guattari, 2003, p. 507). It is adumbral in that it does not have a definitive beginning nor a finite ending, but is rather characterised by foggy peripheries. As a subcutaneous shadow of sonoric haze, it liberates a complexity of interpretive polyphonies (Deleuze & Guattari, 2003, p. 297); and, as a raw and intangible experience, musical listening transforms into a haecceitous hieroglyph of becoming – a metastatically spreading multiplicity within its own span of happening and resonance (Boretz, 2008, p. 68). Approached in this way, no singular experience of music is definitive with respect to any other; each haecceity becomes, a 'strangely relativistic platonic form subsisting exactly, exclusively, and universally within its own boundaries' (Boretz, 2008, p. 76). As a fragment, the liberated splinter of a haecceity – which manifests as a minority text – functions as a component of the larger song of subjective being and becoming (Omry, 2016, p. 108).

For Deleuze and Guattari haecceity offers a conceptual *perpendicularity* that allows for multi-linear fluidity, which fractures the mechanics that underpin more closed and inflexible theoretical approaches to culture and music. In recognising the free play of internal space, the haecceitous and relative duration of a penumbral refrain, enhances the internal dynamics of the fold. Noting Benoit Mandelbrot's (1977, 1983) work on fractals and fractal geometry, Deleuze and Guattari align haecceity with rhizomatic principles.[5] Developed from the Latin term *fractus*, fractal relates to *frangere*, which means 'to break', which is also associated with irregularity and fragmentation (Mandelbrot, 1983, p. 4). For Mandelbrot the natural world does not consist of perfectly aligned or identical linear shapes, such as cones, boxes, or triangles. Instead, clouds, snowflakes, coastlines, and cities are populated and structured around chaotic and rugged terrains; dynamic shapes that manifest as part of an infinite number of possibilities in size, scale, and permutation. Thus, as a strange geometry, fractals articulate and represent fractures and non-uniform shapes in nature and human experience that are, 'grainy, hydralike, in between, pimply, pocky, ramified, seaweedy, strange, tangled, tortuous, wiggly, wispy, wrinkled, and the like' (Mandelbrot, 1983, p. 5). The Mandelbrotian fractal has a visual representation in the form of the Mandelbrot beetle; a computer-generated and aesthetically beautiful shape that produces the resemblance of the body of a beetle. Each of the spiky protuberances that emanate from the circumference of the beetle can be magnified and 'zoomed' in to, which in turn open further and multiple worlds of additional (and infinite) Mandelbrot sets. The Mandelbrot beetle and the associated Mandelbrot set produce a stunning example of multi-directional space and the fractured ingressions that appear within and beyond segmentations of *stabilised* and delineated wholes.

Establishing a connection between music and fractality, Cross (2005) notes that human musical expression frequently engages with fractal properties, whether they be, 'the intricate patterns within a fugue, the choreography of dance, or the play of light and shadow in cloudscapes and landscapes' (Cross, 2005, p. 5). As such, the conceptualisation of human intricacy and difference associated with music-hued haecceities and penumbral refrains, articulate the unpredictable complexity of subjective thought and expression. With this, infringements of external culture, when subjectively encountered, produce inner refractions that mutate beyond the external world. As fractal essences, penumbral refrains – that form in to haecceities – should be understood as constructive deformations of personal knowledge, that manifest as qualitative hieroglyphs. Considered in this way, penumbral refrains crack open shards of elliptical freedom, to reveal an interior world of fractal unpredictability and uniqueness.

Musica penumbra, haecceity, and utopia

A complementary approach to this experimental interpretation of *music as haecceitous encounter*, can be provided by the work of the Marxist utopian philosopher of music Ernst Bloch.[6] Bloch offers his philosophical system as a complex work of gravitational wonder (Jameson, 1971); and suggests that all kinds of culture-work – inclusive of all forms of music – act as utopian conduits. In this way, haecceitous experiences of music manifest as hieroglyphic utopian prompts, that emanate and recur throughout all facets of everyday life. For Bloch, personal musical encounters are important as they agitate life to listen, 'to itself, as a shaped longing and urging in itself, as a song travelling on its own or mingling with others and always portraying invisible human features' (Bloch, 1985, p. 195). For Bloch, the pneumatic fabric of harboured musical sounds sonorically haunts us, and articulates momentary recognitions that *something* is missing (Bloch, 1985, p. 199). To follow Bloch's invitation towards open thinking territories on music and hope, necessitates the awakening of our own subjective, *musica penumbras* and fractal haecceities and to recognise them as nostalgic stories of unfinished futures.[7] Weissberg (1992) informs us that Bloch's work perfectly embodies a provocative and challenging approach to thinking about and engaging with culture and music. By presenting readers with his own personal trove of cultural experiences and memorial connections, Bloch entices people to embark upon similar archaeological ways of thinking; within the context of this chapter, this can be adapted to encourage people to pursue and uncover haecceities and penumbral refrains in the decipherment and recovery of their own fragments of hope. For Bloch, this *Expressionistic* form of personal musical experience, and its adaptive reinterpretation is a purposeful technique, one that can make visible thoughts, connections, and memories that may otherwise remain hidden.

In his essay *Motifs of Concealment*, Bloch (2006) suggests that it is within intense moments of musical *recognition* that we can find our latent selves calling out for revival. Nostalgic echoes that dwell within the hides and fractal interiorities of our penumbras, extending out as an incognito possibility in the form of a minority utopian text. This fruitful incognito refers to a kernel of the human condition that is perpetually incomplete or not-yet-become. For Bloch, the experience of music is therefore seismographic, in that it 'reflects cracks beneath the surface, expresses desires for change, and is synonymous with hoping' (Bloch, 1985, p. 227). Through sonic flashes of astonished possibility, we become prompted to actively daydream beyond the quidditous aspects of ideological and external music-work (Bloch, 2000). By detecting and responding to refracted utopian irruptions, refrains become nudged or prompted to play a part in the unfolding of the fuzzy apparition of a potentially transformative future. Within the context of this chapter, the creative process of recounting and piecing together the sonoric fragments of an excursive penumbral refrain, enables the utopistic hollow space of alternative subjective futures to surface and appear. From within private, subjective worlds, personal catalogues or traces of sonoric fragments emanate as hieroglyphic shards of hope; as fractal and haecceitous shadows of incompleteness they creatively and actively engage with atomised pasts. Musica penumbra therefore hints towards the openness of the future as a utopian gap; an Expressionistic space into which we can discover and divine our own incremental paths, a 'wish-dream applie[d] to a location which is not already present' (Bloch, 1985, p. 217). As haecceities, sonoric striations remind us that something is lacking, and our penumbral refrains uncover this lack clearly. The fractal experience of music therefore harbours 'something dark and thirsty' (Bloch, 1985, p. 197), a dynamic essence of hope, that reminds us that the unfolding of our unmade tomorrows is yet to be arrived at (Moylan, 2000, p. 275).

As a fundamental source of potential transition, the penumbral refrain (as a fractal haecceity) elicits a potency to induce human articulations to visualise and establish subjective dignity in the form of the not-yet (Bloch, 1971).[8] As musical witnesses we encounter the inception and development of own subjective not-yet-conscious and not-yet-become awakenings and journeys. Music-fused haecceities thus harbour penumbral fascinations as personalised sequestrations, musical segments, in the form of hijacked sequences of notes, reinterpreted webs of lyrics and undulating segments of musical meaning. In their most sublime or cosmically purest form, penumbral refrains catalyse the ether of a utopian *something* that cannot be definitively communicated. As an individual and interior experience a haecceic refrain thus provokes wonder and imaginations to daydream beyond the residue of 'Now'.

Within this Blochian context a penumbral refrain can be understood as a personalised vignette, a space that is pregnant with the recognition of the need to remember; not a resigned reminiscence, but a powerful future-oriented form of anagnoretic remembering, with the purpose of 'thinking forward and beyond' the stasis of the past and constraints of the present (Hudson, 1982). Refracted and bespoken shards of sonoric folds thus provide enchanted entrances or extra-ideological openings to the mutant realm of haecceity, in these fleeting and psychically aromatic moments, we are reminded of the mystery of latent possibility (McManus, 2003).

To think and meditate upon the impact of music in this way suggests that there are deep and embedded reasons as to why sonoric folds irrupt and subsequently nudge, shock, and cajole the awakening of astonished secrets. Relative and embryonic hope gestations pang as strange and relative traces; dynamic and untethered point-tracks that sputter an incognito something. Revealing the empty space of the future on the periphery of a music-based haecceity, unfolds chaotic whispers of jubilee, and the restoration of hope for renegade amnesiacs.

Filtered through the Barthesean, Deleuzean, and Blochian theoretical lenses, the minority language that emerges as part of a *penumbral refrain* bleeds in to and textually fuses with the remnant traces and latent material of subjective hope. As collaborative witnesses we reach-in to our subjective haecceities with expressionistic freedom; to produce associative experiences that exude personal creativity. The startling irruptions that emerge from the mystery of musical listening therefore unravel utopian threads of fractal-awakenings.

Beyond external quanta's, the creative human spirit glimmers and murmurs; as hope-detectives, we collect and piece together haecceities as music-utopian clues in pursuit of 'that' which has not yet become. Through the penumbra of musical haecceities the hidden (and revealed) rebuses of personal incompleteness, challenge and facilitate unique characteristics as individual essence and archaeological recovery. Through the personalised and creative process of exploration, wonder-arousing connections arise from music-based trace-awakenings that have the potential to open out towards unseen or forgotten directions. As Bloch informs us, moments of wonder should not be 'ultimately directed to that which has developed but to a question itself, passing through the world, undeveloped and unanswered' (Bloch, 1970). As such, the haecceity of penumbral refrains should be understood as expressionistic and empowering experiences, with the ability to revive past or incomplete aspirations. With, and through, musical listening, we gravitate towards the complexion and openness of hope and the incompleteness of the future. Through the fractal mystery of music we can gaze beyond the demarcated terrain of the present, and learn how to 'sing new songs for tomorrow'; with this, we can evoke renewed visions of different possibilities, and write ourselves in to a utopian text of music that does not-yet exist.

Notes

1 Roland Barthes articulates his liberatory and expressionistic notion of text and polysemy in the essay 'Death of the Author' in *Image, Music, Text* (Barthes, 1977c, pp. 142–148).

2 Deleuze notes that the 'Outside, more distant than any exterior, is 'twisted', 'folded' and 'doubled' by an Inside that is deeper than any interior, and alone creates the possibility of the derived relation between the interior and the exterior' (Deleuze, 2006c, p. 110).

3 Manning (2016) notes that the minor gesture, allied to Gilles Deleuze and Félix Guattari's concept of the minor, 'is the gestural force that opens experience to its potential variation. It does this from within experience itself, activating a shift in tone, a difference in quality. The major is a structural tendency that organises itself according to predetermined definitions of value. The minor is a force that courses through it, unmooring its structural integrity, problematising its normative standards … The minor is a continual variation on experience. It has a mobility not given to the major: its rhythms are not controlled by a pre-existing structure, but open to flux' (Manning, 2016, p. 1).

4 In this sense, rhizomatic expression 'does not crystalise into a unifying form; instead, the expression is a proliferation of different lines of growth. The work resembles crabgrass, a bewildering multiplicity of stems and roots which can cross at any point to form a variety of possible connections. Reading can participate in these connections; a reader makes connections as he reads. He need not interpret and say what the text means; he can discover where passages in the text lead, with what they can be connected. The result is not an interpretation but a map, a tool with which to find a way. The map is the production of an experimental reading' (Deleuze & Guattari, 1983, p. 14).

5 Deleuze and Guattari note, Benoit Mandelbrot's 'fractals' seem to be rhizomatic, in that, 'Fractals are aggregates whose number of dimensions is fractional rather than whole, or else whole but with continuous variation in direction … [M]otion, turbulence, and the sky are "fractals" of this kind. Perhaps this provides us with another way of defining *fuzzy aggregates*' (Deleuze & Guattari, 2003, pp. 486–487). Furthermore, D&G note that rhizomatics, haecceity and fractality are characterised by a, 'fundamental heterogeneity: felt or patchwork … [a] Riemannian space rather than Euclidean space – a continuous variation that exceeds any distribution of constants and variables, the freeing of a line that does not pass between two points' (Deleuze & Guattari, 2003, p. 488).

6   Bloch wrote his major work the 3 volume *The Principle of Hope*, which suggests that dream visions and longings that emerge throughout personal cultural experiences act as initial emotional twinkling of a utopian spirit; existential stirrings of the need and desire to step over or venture beyond (Uberschreiten) the constraints of the immediate, lived moment. Bloch's philosophical style and distinctive prose is inherently difficult to decipher, and his use and definition of utopia is not immediately (at least in a simplistic sense) comparable to other utopian theoretical frameworks. Because of its esoteric, sprawling style, his work fell out of mainstream academic use after his death in 1977; however, there appears to have been a recent resurgence of interest (from the 1990s onwards). The way that Bloch's philosophical style tenuously bridges the wide-ranging and pivotal extremes of the unfolding hope and dignity of humanity, with the chaos of the personal, leaves a difficult space to traverse. Of course, this is not an error or omission on Bloch's part, rather, the reciprocal space between the personal traces of hope-patterns and the unfolding trans-human utopian future is a purposeful gap, an Expressionistic-space. Utopia is a problematic concept – usefully, within Ernst Bloch's philosophical framework, it is assigned the formula of the not-yet, and so, can be understood as consisting of undisclosed hints towards new possibilities on the horizons of tomorrow. Habermas notes that Bloch's analysis and treatment of the notion of utopia 'operates not only with a mere approximation to totalities but out of an anticipatory grasp of these [which] cannot meaningfully be reduced to a differential analysis, nor can the concept of utopia be reduced to the content of regulative ideas' (Habermas, 1983, pp. 75–76).

7   My own work on Bloch has developed the notion of utopia and culture in relation to chaos and fractality; for further reading see Hammond (2012, 2017, 2019); see also Zimmermann (2017) and Zimmermann and Zhang (2017).

8   Wayne Hudson provides a particularly useful definition of Bloch's notion of the not-yet here: 'not yet' may mean 'not so far', in which case it refers to the past as well as to the present. Then 'not yet' may mean 'still not', implying that something expected or envisaged in the past has failed to eventuate. Here the stress falls on the past non-occurrence, and in some cases this failure to eventuate in the past increases the likelihood of a future realisation. This ambiguity is even stronger in German since noch-nicht means both 'still not' and 'not yet'. Or 'not yet' may mean not so far, but 'expected in the future' … the utopian 'not yet' … implies that something is 'conceivable now but not yet possible'' (Hudson, 1982, p. 20).

References

Barthes, R. (1977a). Musica Practica. In R. Barthes (Ed.), *Image, Music, Text* (S. Heath, Trans., pp. 149–154). London: Fontana Press.

Barthes, R. (1977b). From Work to Text. In R. Barthes (Ed.), *Image, Music, Text* (pp. 155–164). London: Fontana Press.

Barthes, R. (1977c). *Image, Music, Text* (S. Heath, Trans.). London: Fontana Press.

Barthes, R. (1978). *A Lovers Discourse* (R. Howard, Trans.). London: Penguin.

Barthes, R. (1991). Listening. In R. Barthes, *The Responsibility of Forms: Critical Essays on Music, Art and Representation* (R. Howard, Trans., pp. 245–260). Berkeley: University of California Press.

Bates, T. (2010). *Duns Scotus and the Problem of Universals*. London: Continuum International Publishing Group.

Bloch, E. (1970). *A Philosophy of the Future*. New York: Herder & Herder.

Bloch, E. (1971). *On Karl Marx* (J. Maxwell, Trans.). New York: Herder & Herder.

Bloch, E. (1985). *Essays on the Philosophy of Music* (P. Palmer, Trans.). Cambridge: Cambridge University Press.

Bloch, E. (2000). *The Spirit of Utopia* (A. A. Nassar, Trans.). Stanford: Stanford University Press.

Bloch, E. (2006). *Traces* (A. A. Nassar, Trans.). Palo Alto: Stanford University Press.

Blumenberg, H. (1993). Light as a Metaphor for Truth: At the Preliminary Stage of Philosophical Concept Formation. In D. M. Levin (Ed.), *Modernity and the Hegemony of Vision* (pp. 30–60). Berkeley: University of California Press.

Boretz, B. (2008). Rainyday Reflections. *Perspectives of New Music, 46*(2), 59–80.

Cross, B. (2005). *The Fractal Imagination: New Resources for Conceptualising Creativity*. Edinburgh University, Centre for Educational Sociology. Edinburgh: Edinburgh University.

Cseres, J. (2017). Musica Practica according to Roland Barthes. *Musicologica Brunensia, 52*(1). doi: http://dx.doi.org/10.5817/MB2017-1-14

Deleuze, G. (1997). *Essays Critical and Clinical* (D. W. Smith & M. A. Greco, Trans.). Minneapolis: University of Minnesota.

Deleuze, G. (2001). *Difference and Repetition* (P. Patton, Trans.). London: Continuum.

Deleuze, G. (2006a). Making Inaudible Forces Audible. In *Two Regimes of Madness* (A. Hodges & M. Taormina, Trans., pp. 156–160). Cambridge: MIT Press.

Deleuze, G. (2006b). *The Fold* (T. Conley, Trans.). London: Continuum.

Deleuze, G. (2006c). *Foucault* (S. Hand, Trans.). Minneapolis: University of Minnesota Press.

Deleuze, G., & Guattari, F. (1983). What Is a Minor Literature? (R. Brinkley, Ed.) *Mississippi Review, 11*(3), 13–33.

Deleuze, G., & Guattari, F. (1986). *Kafka toward a Minor Literature* (D. Polan & R. Bensmaia, Trans.). Minneapolis: University of Minnesota Press.

Deleuze, G., & Guattari, F. (2003). *A Thousand Plateaus: Capitalism and Schizophrenia* (B. Massumi, Trans.). London: Continuum.

Deleuze, G., & Guattari, F. (2005). *A Thousand Plateaus: Capitalism and*

Duffy, M. (2017). Learning Assemblages: Re-sounding Place and Mapping the Affects of Sound. In P. Moisala, L. M. Tiainen & H. Vèaèatèainen (Eds.), *Musical Encounters with Deleuze and Guattari* (pp. 189–203). London: Bloomsbury Academic.

Gingerich, S. D. (2008). Telling (in) the Half-Light: Mimetic Poetics and Juan Benet's En la penumbra. *Hispania, 91*(3), 569–578.

Habermas, J. (1983). Ernst Bloch: A Marxist Schelling (1980). In J. Habermas (Ed.), *Philosophical-Political Profiles* (F. G. Lawrence, Trans., pp. 61–77). London: Heinemann.

Hammond, C. A. (2012). Towards a Neo-Blochian Theory of Complexity, Hope and Cinematic Utopia. Lancaster: Lancaster University (PhD Thesis).

Hammond, C. A. (2017). *Hope, Utopia and Creativity in Higher Education: Pedagogical Tactics for Alternative Futures*. London: Bloomsbury Academic.

Hammond, C.A. (2019). Folds, Fractals and Bricolages for Hope: Some Conceptual and Pedagogical Tactics for a Creative Higher Education. In P. Gibbs & A. Peterson (Eds.), *Higher Education and Hope: Institutional, Pedagogical and Personal Possibilities* (pp. 135–155). London: Palgrave Macmillan.

Hudson, W. (1982). *The Marxist Philosophy of Ernst Bloch*. London: Macmillan.

Jameson, F. (1971). A Marxist Hermeneutic III: Ernst Bloch and the Future. In F. Jameson (Ed.), *Marxism and Form: Twentieth-Century Dialectical Theories of Literature* (pp. 116–156). Princeton: Princeton University Press.

Jeongwon, J., & Song, S.H. (2002). Roland Barthes' "Text" and Aleatoric Music: Is "The Birth of the Reader" The Birth of the Listener? *Muzikologija, 2*, 263–281. doi: https://doi.org/10.2298/MUZ0202263J

Kepler, J. (2000). *Optics: Paralipomena to Witelo & Optical Part of Astronomy* (W. H. Donahue, Trans.). Sant Fe: Green Lion Press.

Mandelbrot, B. (1977). *Fractals: Form, chance, and dimension*. San Francisco: W. H. Freeman & Co.

Mandelbrot, B. (1983). *The Fractal Geometry of Nature*. New York: W. H. Freeman & Co.

Mandelbrot, B. (1999). *Multifractals and 1/f Noise: Wild Self-Affinity in Physics* (vol. Selecta Volume N). New York: Springer.

Manning, E. (2016). *The Minor Gesture*. Durham: Duke University Press.

McManus, S. (2003). Fabricating the Future: Becoming Bloch's Utopians. *Utopian Studies, 14*.

Merz, J., & Merz, S. (2017). Occupying the Ontological Penumbra: Towards a Postsecular and Theologically Minded Anthropology. *Religions, 8*(80), 2–17. doi: https://doi.org/10.3390/rel8050080

Moylan, T. (2000). *Scraps of the Untainted Sky*. Virginia: University of Virginia Press.

Omry, K. (2016). Bodies and Digital Discontinuities: Posthumanism, Fractals, and Popular Music in the Digital Age. *Science Fiction Studies, 43*(1), 104–122.

Rosenkrantz, G. (1993). *Haecceity: On Ontological Essay*. Dordrecht: Kluwer Academic Publishers.

Scotus, D. (1963). *Philosophical Writings* (A. Wolter, Ed. & A. Wolter, Trans.). Edinburgh: Thomas Nelson & Sons Ltd.

Weissberg, L. (1992). Philosophy and the Fairy Tale: Ernst Bloch as Narrator. *New German Critique, 55*, 21–44.

Wortel, E. (2011). From History to Haecceity: Spatial Reframings of the Past in Post-Heritage Cinema. *Alphaville: Journal of Film and Screen Media, 2*, 1–16.

Zimmermann, R. E. (2017). Experimentum Mundi sive adumbratio. In R. E. Zimmermann (Ed.), *Ernst Bloch: Das Prinzip Hoffnung* (pp. 81–98). Berlin: Walter de Gruyter.

Zimmermann, R. E. & Zhang, X. (2017). Information and Meaning in Deterministic Chaos: A Blochian Perspective. *Digitalisation for a Sustainable Society* (p. 247). MDPI Proceedings, Gothenberg. doi: https://doi.org/10.3390/IS4SI-2017-04090

5 Policing Death

Indonesian Death Metal Music and Alleged or Apparent Criminality

Kieran James

Introduction

In his article on East Jakarta band Siksa Kubur, Dennis William Lee (2018) notes that both Punk and Heavy Metal music were labeled as the music of working-class youth and social outcasts during the Soeharto era. A key event was the riot following a Metallica concert in Jakarta in 1993. This viewpoint is probably still widespread today. The focus of most of this chapter is the Death Metal community of Bandung, West Java (a provincial, mountainous city of 2.5 million people located 115 kilometers south-east of Jakarta). The Bandung scene, hegemonic throughout Indonesia, including remote East Kalimantan, Sulawesi, and Sumatra, is recognized widely as the largest scene in the world. Man, the vocalist of Jasad, told the author that the city had 128 active Death Metal bands on 24 February 2011. This is even more remarkable as Death Metal is the most musically-extreme subgenre and is only one of the number of subgenres within Heavy Metal music. Other important subgenres include Black Metal, deathcore, grindcore, goregrind, hardcore, metalcore, Power Metal, Thrash Metal, and traditional Heavy Metal.

The peak years of the Bandung Death Metal scene were arguably 2009–2013. The scene has fragmented and matured in recent years as older musicians become progressively less active and younger musicians and fans either choose more modern subgenres or continue without strong connections to the pioneers. There has also been a notable shift towards dedicated Islamic religious devotion among musicians and fans alike. Teguh Prasetyo, of the bands Interfectorment and Digging Up, told the author how around half of the fans from the scene's peak years, have left the scene for religious reasons, while one-quarter (i.e., one-half of the one-half) no longer listen to any Death Metal in their personal lives.

History of Bandung Death Metal scene

The Bandung Death Metal scene[1] is known, throughout Indonesia and overseas, for its size; dedication and commitment (to the Death Metal subgenre in particular); extreme self-confidence; professionalism; hierarchical

DOI: 10.4324/9781003186410-5

nature; strong and cohesive networks of merchandise shops, road crews, recording studios, record labels, artists, and tattoo stores; a large number of talented and motivated underground musicians; and high levels of organization (Baulch, 2007; Hutabarat & Kusumah, n.d.; James & Walsh, 2015, 2019; Prasetyo, 2017; Wallach, 2008). It is associated with a lower-middle-class/working-class district in the outer-eastern suburbs called Ujung Berung (or informally 'Ujungbronx') where most of the foundation bands originated in the 1990s. Hutabarat and Kusumah (n.d., p. 3) writes that 'Ujung Berung is the symbol of underground movement in Indonesia,' and, generally, this statement would be acknowledged as valid by metalheads throughout Indonesia. The Ujung Berung community's marketing and self-confidence generated unparalleled momentum and these forces worked in tandem with the obvious artistic talent of the leading early bands. The legendary Ujung Berung bands were formed in the following years: Jasad: 1990, Forgotten: 1994, Burgerkill: 1995, Injected Sufferage: 1995, Disinfected: 1997, Jihad: 1999, Undergod: 2004, Bleeding Corpse: 2006, and Turbidity: 2008. The famous underground festival *Bandung Berisik* 1 was first held in 1995 (Prasetyo, 2017, p. 196). According to Teguh Prasetyo (no relation to the music scholar Frans Ari Prasetyo), bassist of Interfectorment and Digging Up, the peak years of the Bandung Death Metal scene were 2009–2013.

Andy Bennett (2002) explored the Canterbury Sound concept whereby certain bands which emerged out of Canterbury, England 30 or 40 years ago are now venerated by online enthusiasts from around the world who try to link the sound with the city of Canterbury and myths of 'pastoral Englishness.' Unlike other sounds, such as Motown, the Philadelphia Sound, and the Seattle Sound, these bands had little in common sonically, and the sound had no real link to the city. However, in recent years, CD promoters and record shops in Canterbury have joined together with online enthusiasts to fuel the myth of the importance of the sound and its city links and context. Bandung Death Metal is a similar myth or mythscape (Bennett, 2002, p. 89), with Ujung Berung being a mythical locality of underground values, known and revered throughout all of Indonesia's metal scenes including those of remote East Kalimantan and Sumatra. Similarly, Ujung Berung is associated with a particular sound (the Suffocation-Disgorge USA Brutal Death Metal style of scene pioneers Jasad). Other pioneer bands play in Brutal Death Metal style too, such as Forgotten and Jihad, with only minor sonic variations. The myth of Ujung Berung allows Bandung bands to headline in other Indonesian cities, almost as a matter of course, but non-Bandung bands rarely receive the same treatment when they play in Bandung.[2] This has fed into creating some resentment towards the Bandung scene from other cities. The myth of Bandung as a center for arts and culture in Indonesia, dating back decades, has fed into the Ujung Berung myth but only in a way similar to how English punks took advantage of, but also subverted (and reinvigorated), earlier English rock, glam, and mod traditions.

Ujung Berung, the bands and the community, 'tap into familiar local imagery and mobilise existing loyalties within new frameworks and settings' (Hatley, 2012, p. 28), as we hope that this part-chapter on the Ujung Berung Death Metal community will demonstrate.

Indonesian Death Metal music and criminality

In this section, I will explore alleged connections existing in the minds of Indonesian police and elite persons about the alleged connections between Death Metal fandom and criminality. In Bandung a major event in the history of the scene occurred in 2008 when 11 fans were crushed to death at an album launch held by the Bandung metalcore band. The reasons for the sad deaths were failings in building design and construction, to allow for proper exits, and the carelessness of the staff managing the venue on the night. However, the local police assigned blame to Death Metal music and to the band itself. As a result, Beside was perceived to be a 'dangerous band,' along with Death Metal act, Jihad (because its lyrics explore Islamic theology), and hip-hop group Homicide (source for the 'dangerous band' comment: Agrog, ex-Beside vocalist, interview with author, 18 May 2018). It became very difficult for a number of years to hold shows and festivals in Bandung City proper, and, for the band Beside, it was yet more difficult again. More and more shows were held in remote countryside areas in private houses and garages. I attended one such show when the young Bandung band Bloodgush headlined at a Sunday afternoon show at Cililin, three hours' drive out from Bandung, on 27 February 2011. The audience was around 150 to 200 teenagers (about 10–15% being female fans), who appeared at and departed from the idyllic rural setting mostly via motorbike. The bands played in an enclosed garage, owned by a private house, approximately 15 meters long by 7 meters wide. About 10 meters from the garage was the house itself. Attendees were able to enter the house one by one to use the toilet and the members of Bloodgush were able to relax for an hour after their set in the living room of the family's home.

On another occasion, on 1 April 2012, there was a one-day festival in the countryside outside Bandung. Approximately ten bands were scheduled to appear with the first beginning around noon and the last beginning around 8:00 p.m. It was a mixed-genre show with most bands being Death Metal but there were also one or two Punk and Hardcore bands. Because of the mix of bands, about 20% of the attendees wore Punk regalia, while the remainder wore Death Metal merchandise. The crowd was around 200 to 300. In mid-afternoon, around 4:00 p.m., a group of about 30 policemen arrived and went into the venue to tell the Event Organizer (EO) that they were cancelling the festival. I can recall the fans of Bandung hardcore band, Outright, pouring out of the door with disappointment and shock etched upon their teenaged faces. The police then retreated to one far, rear corner of the carpark and watched the crowd disperse. There was no violence or even physical contact. The police allowed the metalheads to maintain their own 'face' and self-respect by allowing them to leave the compound at their own pace. The metalheads acted out their role in the drama by ignoring the police and 'pretending' that they were all leaving voluntarily. In Indonesia, with its history of police brutality, it is always wisest to humbly accept the setbacks of the moment and live to fight another day. Later on, Man of Jasad told us that he believed that if he had been there, he would have been able to resolve the problems with the police. (His band had been due to headline, but he had not been at the venue when the police arrived). Bobby Rock, the tall and genial vocalist of Bleeding Corpse, was cool in the crisis and spent time cheerfully chatting with young fans at the venue that afternoon until the last possible moment. The car containing Bobby, Bobby's wife, and me was the last to depart the compound. It was a blessing in disguise for these fans as, in normal circumstances; they may not have had the chance to chat casually with Bobby.

Maila Stivens (2018) focuses on the gendering of the contemporary social movement in Australia which aims to assist and advocate for asylum seekers. She effectively contrasts the militarized perspective and actions of the Australian government, backed up by its chosen ideology of national security, with the women who attempt to show hospitality to asylum seekers through motherly and feminine images and support. Stivens emphasizes the women-inspired groups' 'affective and embodied politics,' which includes 'intense feelings of protective maternal rage at the Australian state's asylum regime,' and argues that this politics is 'instrumental in producing spaces of cosmopolitan hospitality' (Fitzgerald & Stivens, 2018, p. 82) as a 'situated ethical cosmopolitanism' (Stivens, 2018, p. 92).

As another example of maternal rage or maternal depression, at the April 2012 festival mentioned above, the promising young Bandung band Humiliation was due to play but was prevented from doing so by the police interruption. One of the police personnel was a policewoman who was also the mother of 21-year-old Adam, vocalist of Humiliation. When most of the attendees had left or were in the process of leaving the compound, we discovered Adam's mother – she had been sitting crying in her car. She had had no power to change the police's decision to cancel the festival. At that moment her motherly pride in hoping to watch her son perform dominated over or outweighed her policewoman role – she was torn apart by maternal rage and disappointment. Perhaps because of her gender in a patriarchal society, none of the other police personnel seemed bothered by her distress, which she was probably trying to hide from them by sitting in her car. Perhaps the very act of sitting in her car was her personal rebellion. In my experience, in Indonesia, parental pride over children's achievements and efforts is the dominant parental attitude towards Heavy Metal musicians whereas, by contrast, religious, political, and community leaders, with no 'skin in the game,' often show apathy or hostility.

A famous example of police persecution of Heavy Metal people was the case of the owner of a 'distro' (merchandise store) selling Heavy Metal recordings and merchandise inside the Blok M shopping complex in suburban South Jakarta (Anonymous, 2016; Coconuts Jakarta, 2016; Vallecillo, 2016; Wijaya, 2016). The communist sickle-and-hammer symbol is still an illegal symbol in Indonesia and the nation's political leaders have never apologized over the murder of about one million Indonesian communists in 1965–1966. The shop was selling, amongst other merchandise, a T-shirt depicting the logo of German Thrash Metal band Kreator and a hammer-and-sickle. The offending image had been downloaded by the store-owner and sent to a factory in Bandung to produce 60 T-shirts, i.e., this was not official licensed band merchandise (but the design did come from Kreator). This T-shirt attracted the attention of the police, and they paraded the 'offensive' shirt in front of the media. The arrest can be interpreted as 'moral panic' and an attempt to scapegoat the store-owner and make an example of him for others (although the local police chief later backtracked and admitted that it was just a band T-shirt and not incitement to treason). What is interesting and important is that Kreator is only vaguely left-wing in terms of being environmentalist and pro-Third World empowerment and dissent in the face of corrupt regimes. The band has never been communist, and it has never had pro-communist lyrics. Note that this was not a major music chain – it was a small operation set up by a local fan. The police attention for him was the stuff of nightmares. The popularity of this German band in Indonesia (bypassing the hegemonic UK-US axis) also showcases the 'grounded' and 'rooted' cosmopolitanism (Araujo, 2018; Dyer, 2018; Fitzgerald & Stivens, 2018; Pardy, 2018; Stivens, 2018) evident in Indonesian metal scenes.

Recently in Iran, a Death Metal band, Arsames (est. 2002), faced government persecution for allegedly playing 'satanic music' and for being allegedly against the Islamic government (Pasbani, 2020). The band made bail and was subject to the threat of 15 years' imprisonment. In updated news it was later revealed that the band members had fled the country. The Indonesian metal communities are fortunate that their difficulties have never been quite this extreme.

Globalization and discontinuities – The case of Sickles from Madura Island

The case of Sickles raises a lot of important issues connected to contemporary globalization and identity formation. It also allows us to see how 'grounded' and 'rooted' cosmopolitanism (which is not bourgeois or corporate) operates in the global Death Metal Underground and has done since the days of tape-trading in the 1980s (Kahn-Harris, 2007; Mudrian, 2004). It also highlights the impact of neo-colonialism, which positions young Indonesian men and women at the bottom of a global hierarchy. They sometimes need to and/or want to leave their home cities in search of employment, which means that bands are frequently disrupted, put on-hold, declared inactive, or split up. This has adverse implications for the cohesion and mood of the scene and the scene is forced to adapt from within to respond to temporary setbacks. Usually, scenes eventually recover as younger people rise up to take the place of departed musicians.

Madura Island is a quiet, socially- and politically-conservative island off the coast of East Java. It is reached via a causeway bridge from the cosmo-politan mega-city of Surabaya, which has a large and well-established metal scene rivaling that of Bandung for size, reach, and sophistication.[3] Unlike Bandung, where the Death Metal genre is hegemonic, Surabaya's scene has a good mix of genres but the main genre is Power Metal, which is a variant of traditional Heavy Metal with its sung, rather than growled or screamed, vocals, and musical virtuosity. Heavy Metal's roots in Surabaya, according to Valerian guitarist Dimas Bramantyo (in conversation with the author), can be traced to the Hard-Rock music which visiting servicemen and tour-ists brought to the East Javanese port-city from the 1950s through to the 1980s.

The Madura town adjacent to Surabaya is Bangkalan (population 95,000), and the Madura Heavy Metal community is centered in Bangkalan although there are bands based in other cities too. Madura Island is a very religious Islamic place with a number of Islamic schools and colleges being located there. Nearly all girls and women wear the *hijab*, which is not the case in Surabaya. It maintains an identity and feeling very different from Surabaya, although the awareness of cosmopolitan and potentially corrupt-ing Surabaya, just over the bridge, never goes away. It is difficult to obtain alcohol in Madura and in my two trips there I stuck to non-alcoholic drinks. Members of the Surabaya metal community sometimes visit Bangkalan, usually on day-trips, and they encourage and mentor the younger Madura bands. The scene in Madura probably numbered not more than 50 active members as in December 2014 (most of whom were band members in one or more bands) and their ages were very young with most members being aged late-teens to early-twenties. As in December 2014, Madura had seven or eight active bands across all genres, including Ant Killers (deathcore), Bull Race (hardcore), Kremasi (metalcore), Mutilation Aggression (Death Metal, from Kamal), Rajam (War Metal), Sickles (Death Metal), and Tyrannical Mirror (deathcore).

Given Madura's religious and conservative culture, it is interesting to note that the Madura metal scene members are also relatively careful, restrained, polite, and cautious. They do not have long hair; they rarely wear band T-shirts featuring artwork of gore, blood, and murder; and they do not wear jackets with band patches on them (referred to as 'battle jackets'). They need to adapt to their surroundings and fit in socially so as to go to college and high-school, secure employment, and/or find marriage partners. They are very aware that only part of their life is lived within the scene (Kahn-Harris,

2007), and the rest is lived outside of it. The large proportion of bands playing more modern (post-2000) styles of metal music, including metalcore and
deathcore, reflects the youthfulness of the band members and the lack of
scene numbers and infrastructure (which precludes mini-scenes being created for each subgenre).

The band Sickles (pronounced 'Sick-less') was formed in 2012 by brothers
Arie (guitar) and Rony (bass). The band released a seven-track EP *Series
Elite Disaster* in March 2014 (limited to 500 copies). Its style of technically
intricate Brutal Death Metal, with lyrics about traditional Maduranese
history, and a couple of innovative video-clips, began to win underground
attention throughout Indonesia and overseas. Haidir was the drummer (still
in high-school) and Irsyad was on vocals. Arie was about 21-years-old and
Rony about 18 in 2014. The underground music promoter and Death Metal
aficionado, Andrew Talbot aka Andrew Sick of Sick Reviews, Canada,
began promoting and supporting Sickles through social-media and did a
review of the band's EP. The band members – Rony (bass), Irsyad (vocals),
Haidir (drums), and Arie (guitar) – were overjoyed to get respect and validation from an aficionado from a faraway Western country.

I first visited the house in Bangkalan where Arie and Rony live with their
mother in January 2014. One room is reserved for a small merchandise shop
which sells band T-shirts and CDs. The two brothers had told their mother
that an author/journalist was coming to visit them from Australia. Their
mother refused to believe them until I arrived on their doorstep, accompa-
nied by several members of the Surabaya scene, including a man and woman
who acted as interpreter for me in band interviews. Again, we saw maternal
pride as Arie and Rony's mother was amazed that a white-foreigner would
come to their remote town to visit her sons. This was like a validation for
their musical efforts, and the support from Andrew Sick, although only ever
virtual, was just as meaningful and appreciated. Andrew Sick had to face
racism and Islamophobia by promoting an Indonesian band to his Canadian
and global audience, but he stuck to his convictions and ethical beliefs and
refused to back down in his support of Sickles. He encountered the common
attitudes of 'what good can come from such a global backwater?' and 'how
can religious people from a Muslim country play such a rebellious and coun-
tercultural type of music?' Andrew Sick, as mentioned, never gave up in his
support for Sickles and other Indonesian bands online even in the face of
entrenched and consistent racism, Islamophobia, indifference, and apathy.
The validation from Canada and Australia raised Sickles' subcultural capital (Kahn-Harris, 2007; Thornton, 1995) significantly within Indonesian
underground scenes and put the whole Madura scene on the map. Although
veteran War Metal band, Rajam, had a large underground cult following
throughout Indonesia, it was the younger Sickles which had broken through
to international audiences. And Yayak, mastermind of Rajam, in humble
manner, was very quick to acknowledge and support Sickles too rather than
being beset by jealousy.

However, in September 2016, Irsyad found work on an international cruise-ship. His Facebook page showed pictures of this smiling Indonesian side-by-side with his workmates, dressed in light-blue overalls, either on board ship or at various overseas destinations. Sickles was badly affected – it only played occasional shows thereafter, with a guest vocalist (the vocalist of Ant Killers), and no new recordings have been released (source: Metal Archives). Rony joined forces with Ghofur Al Hikam (guitarist) in a new Death Metal venture, Decaying Flesh (source: author's interview with Rony of Decaying Flesh, 3 April 2017). He also plays bass in Unscarred with guitarist Dhidit Ratt (ex-Jagal) and this band has a dual Madura-Surabaya identity (source: author's interview with Dhidit Ratt of Unscarred, 12 September 2018). This example shows Irsyad's desire or need to get a job which would take him away from Madura and the negative impact this had on his band and his local scene. Rony 'graduated' to forming a band with a leading Surabaya guitarist and has found his own form of success there. With support from Swallow Vomit Productions of Thailand, Rony continues to operate at an international level. Both Decaying Flesh and Unscarred have released one studio album apiece.

The Sickles' page on Metal Archives lists the band as 'active' and lists the classic line-up of Arie, Rony, Irsyad, and Haidir as still the current line-up. Rony told me on 23 October 2020 that the band is presently preparing a new single. 'Killed by a Cruise-ship' (a play on the Motörhead song 'Killed by Death') is an appropriate summary headline for the whole Sickles' saga.

Conclusion

This chapter has revealed how vast, diverse, sophisticated, and well-developed the Heavy Metal scenes of Bandung and Surabaya are (although in the latter case it has been asserted rather than demonstrated due to space constraints). Police and politicians fail to understand the nature of the musical communities, or the subcultural discourses and practices involved, because they are so full of myth-making and symbolism and are essentially a movement imported from the West, but adapted to suit local needs, inclinations, and preferences. The persecution of the South Jakarta shop-owner looks ludicrous to outside observers and the governments need to reflect on why they still fear a symbol which lost its power in world politics 30 to 40 years ago. Their lack of knowledge is also evident given that they are unaware that Kreator is only vaguely left-wing in the sense of vaguely supporting Third World liberation movements and street-based activism in the face of (generally unnamed) oppressive regimes. The Indonesian police fell into the beginner's trap of conforming to Kreator's prior expectations of Third World police-states rather than proving the band wrong through tolerance and benevolence.

However, the festival cancelled in April 2012 does at least show the police being willing to allow the crowd to leave at its own speed in a way which allowed for face-saving. Despite this, the festival posed no moral danger to anyone in the audience and deprived many young local teenagers of some harmless enjoyment and social interaction. It may be taking a step too far to say that the attendees were 'criminalized,' as no-one was arrested, and it was more a matter of the local police wanting to save their own face and demonstrate their own importance. Youth-based subcultural movements of foreign origin were viewed as suspicious and nerve-wracking. However, for Adam's mother, she was depressed not to see her son in action onstage – her maternal role dominated her policewoman's role, at that precise moment, and this theme is common throughout Indonesian musical scenes. Parental pride in a child's achievements trumps generalized and impersonal 'moral' or 'religious' panics.

The discussion of Sickles shows that the Madura scene is careful, restrained, polite, and low-profile as reflecting an isolated, religious, and socially conservative island community, which perceives itself as continually under threat from cosmopolitan and hedonistic Surabaya over the causeway. The Madura metalheads are very young and there are few fans that don't actually play in bands. They are shorthaired, wear plain black T-shirts minus gruesome artwork, and avoid patched battle-jackets (at least in 2014 this was the case). They want to fly under-the-radar so that they can focus on their craft and continue to function in the non-metal world where they need to attend schools and colleges, hold down jobs, and/or find girlfriends and future wives.

The case of Sickles shows the importance of global underground networks, and we see a grounded and rooted working-class cosmopolitanism in action. But Sickles is active in name only now and the band is forced to wait for Irsyad to become available again. Meanwhile Rony joins forces with Surabaya musicians, and he has 'graduated' from the Bangkalan milieu, whilst retaining his roots in the Bangkalan community. The support received from the day-tripping Surabaya metalheads has been vitally important in building up and nurturing the Madura scene, as vital in its own way as the Canadian Sick Reviews connection. Surabaya musicians, such as Dimas Bramantyo, Daniel Natjaard, Verrel Valerian, Dwi Yudha, and Ms Dhinie (ex-Valerian) deserve respect and gratitude for their continued efforts to mentor and support the Bangkalan scene members. Sickles' achievements were and are formidable for a young band fighting the odds in such a remote and conservative place. Death Metal is a subculture which encourages youth to aim for musical proficiency, as part of a local scene of enduring bonds and which connects, through individuals, shops, studios, radio DJs, travelers, and touring bands, to a network of scenes which spans the country and beyond. No-one is ever really alone.

Notes

1   Death Metal and Death Metal people remain hegemonic in the Bandung metal scene in terms of their domination of institutions, discourses, and practices.
2   Two established Surabaya-based musicians, Dimas Bramantyo of Valerian and Endro Wibowo of Jagal, expressed their frustration about this situation to the author on 8 December 2014.

3 The 5.4-kilometer-long Suramadu Bridge (Indonesian: *Jembatan Suramadu*), also known as the Surabaya-Madura Bridge, connects Bangkalan to the mainland of Java.

References

Anonymous. (2016, May 9). Indonesian store owners arrested over Kreator T-shirt featuring "communism" symbol. *Blabbermouth*. Retrieved from https://www. blabbermouth.net/news/

Araujo, N. (2018). Engendering cosmopolitanism: Gendered narratives of instability and agency. *Women's Studies International Forum, 67*(1), 102–109.

Baulch, E. (2007). *Making scenes: Reggae, punk, and death metal in 1990s Bali*. Durham, NC: Duke University Press.

Bennett, A. (2002). Music, media and urban mythscapes: A study of the 'Canterbury Sound'. *Media, Culture and Society, 24*(1), 87–100.

Coconuts Jakarta. (2016, May 9). Police arrest owner of Blok M store for selling heavy metal t-shirts with communist symbol. Retrieved from https://coconuts. co/jakarta/news/

Dyer, M. (2018). Ungrounded cosmopolitanism: Intersections of moral responsibility and gender in environmental activism in rural Solomon Islands. *Women's Studies International Forum, 67*(1), 128–135.

Fitzgerald, R.P., & Stivens, M. (2018). Editorial for special section "Gendering cosmopolitanisms: Recognition, belonging and difference". *Women's Studies International Forum, 67*(1), 80–84.

Hatley, B. (2012). Performing identity and community in Indonesia in modern times. *ACCESS: Critical Perspectives on Communication, Cultural and Policy Studies, 31*(2), 27–38.

Hutabarat, F., & Kusumah, I.R.A. (n.d.). Market development using community shared values: The case of Burgerkill. Retrieved from http://www.creativeconference.co.za/wp-content/uploads/2016/01/Felencia-Kimung-Paper-revised. pdf

James, K., & Walsh, R. (2015). Bandung rocks, Cibinong shakes: Economics and applied ethics within the Indonesian death-metal community. *Musicology Australia, 37*(1), 27–46.

James, K., & Walsh, R. (2019). Religion and heavy metal music in Indonesia. *Popular Music, 38*(2), 276–297.

Kahn-Harris, K. (2007). *Extreme metal: Music and culture on the edge*. London and New York, NY: Berg.

Lee, D.W. (2018). 'Negeri seribu bangsa': Musical hybridization in contemporary Indonesian death metal. *Metal Music Studies, 4*(3), 531–548.

Mudrian, A. (2004). *Choosing death: The improbable history of death metal and grindcore*. Los Angeles, CA: Feral House.

Pardy, M. (2018). Transnational feminisms and cosmopolitan feelings. *Women's Studies International Forum, 67*(1), 94–101.

Pasbani, R. (2020, August 1). Iranian metal band Arsames arrested, sentenced to 15 years in prison for playing "satanic" music. *Metal Injection*. Retrieved from https://metalinjection.net/metal-crimes

Prasetyo, F.A. (2017). Punk and the city: A history of punk in Bandung. *Punk & Post-Punk, 6*(2), 189–211.

Stivens, M. (2018). Gendering cosmopolitanisms: Hospitality and the asylum seeking other. *Women's Studies International Forum, 67*(1), 85–93.

Thornton, S. (1995). *Club cultures: Music, media and sub-cultural capital.* Cambridge: Polity Press.

Vallecillo, A. (2016, May 9). Record store owners arrested over Kreator t-shirt showing communist symbol. *Metal Insider.* Retrieved from https://www.metal-insider.net/

Wallach, J. (2008). *Modern noise, fluid genres: Popular music in Indonesia, 1997–2001.* Madison, WI: University of Wisconsin Press.

Wijaya, C.A. (2016, May 10). Police release two people caught selling hammer and sickle t-shirts. *The Jakarta Post.* Retrieved from https://www.thejakartapost.com/news/2016/05/10/

6 Decriminalising Rap Beat by Beat

Two Questions in Search of Answers

Lambros Fatsis

Introduction

Rap music is variously imagined, talked about, personified and policed through narratives that translate its imagery and lyrical content into evidence of gratuitous violence and rampant misogyny. Condemning an entire music genre and the broader Afro-diasporic culture(s) from which rap emerges, however, tells us more about the politics of description than the defining character(istics) of what is being described. Such offhanded dismissals of rap music (sub)culture(s), therefore, reveal how the mainstream public, scholarly and penal imagination shrink-wraps rap in unquestioned stock responses – rather than doing justice to its artistic nuance, cultural context and sexual politics. This is not to justify, deny or condone any of the violence and misogyny of much commercial(ised) rap. Rather, it is to stress that this is *not what all rap is* or that this is *all that rap is*. Contrary to popular mythology, criminological sophistry, bad press and racialised state-sanctioned violence that routinely criminalise rap(pers), this chapter argues that selectively criminalising rap for (some of) its socially harmful, politically dubious and aesthetically repugnant content does violence to factual accuracy, Black cultural literacy or political education into criminal (in)justice. To address such accusations head-on, the remainder of this text confronts such controversies over the sexual and criminal justice politics of rap music in the form of two questions: (i) isn't it misogynistic? and (ii) isn't it violent? In so doing, a considered reply is attempted to rescue debates on the misogyny and violence in rap from headline-grabbing sensationalism. What is offered instead, is a discussion that rejects the racialisation of misogyny and violence by particularising both in Black music genres and decries the criminalisation of rap; without pretending that such imagery in rap doesn't exist or shouldn't be opposed. Rather, the argument that is advanced here stresses that casting rap out as inherently misogynistic and violent; exonerates the dominant white, patriarchal, heteronormative social order that creates hierarchies of gender, race, class and sexuality that are (pre)served by the very criminal legal institutions that mark Black music genres like rap as 'criminal'. Instead of blaming rap music for the racist gendered state

DOI: 10.4324/9781003186410-6

violence that is otherwise normalised and legitimised within mainstream socio-political culture, criminological scholarship and law enforcement agencies, what follows is an invitation to decriminalise rap; directing our suspicion towards wider socio-political realities to better understand and respond to violence and misogyny – in ways that do not summon forms of creative expression to stand trial for harms that are created in other areas of social and political life.

Isn't it misogynistic?

Accusations of misogyny incriminate rap music, pointing at imagery and lyrics that portray women in offensive, objectifying and derogatory ways. Such chilling representations of male domination over women – littered with nauseating references to 'bitches', 'hoes' (=whores) and 'pussy' – disparage women as sexual(ised) male property, in ways that bear all the hallmarks of sexist patriarchal violence. Listening to, writing about or even defending rap against its discriminatory suppression by the criminal legal system, therefore, inevitably involves accounting for the genre's affront to gender(ed) justice. Calling rap out for its embrace of ideologies of male dominance, however, also carries the danger of singling it out as the worst or only offender, while also slipping into language that racialises gendered violence – when it selectively identifies it in forms of Black cultural expression. This is not to say that *all* critiques of rap fall into such a rhetorical trap, but to stress that this *is* a reflex response to the genre in popular and scholarly denunciations of it. Yet, recognising the perils of essentialising Black popular culture to attack its repellent misogyny neither exonerates rap, nor does it silence critiques against it. Rather, it points to the possibility of conducting analysis and espousing politics that refuse to be complicit with *both* sexism and racism in the battle against gendered and racialised violence. Encouraging such an approach is a difficult, complicated, vexing and anxious endeavour, since rap devotees and feminist critics see their cultural and sexual politics collide.

This chapter argues against such a divide to point out that it is entirely possible to oppose rap's misogyny, without unfairly blaming it on Black popular culture (alone). Challenging the broader racist, a hetero-patriarchal socio-cultural and political context that harms those who are gendered and racialised as deserving targets of racial and gender violence, the remainder of this section insists that the misogyny that is abhorred in rap is not qualitatively different too – nor does it spring from an altogether different cultural soil than the misogyny that is otherwise overlooked, ignored, normalised, legitimised, excused and rationalised in other spheres of social life. This should be a fairly obvious point to make, yet the passions that such debates stir steer us away from a unified rejection of the 'metaphysics of white supremacist capitalist patriarchy' (hooks, 2006: 7) that divert our attention and divide us into warring camps – where a united front is needed instead. Drawing on Black feminist scholarship and those aligned with its politics, the discussion that follows revolves around three related questions: what kind of misogyny does rap broadcast? where does it come from? and what logics are used to oppose it?

The *first* question challenges us to clarify whether there is a specific kind of misogyny that pervades rap that differs markedly in character from other manifestations of it in dominant or mainstream culture. If rap's misogyny is different or worse, then the alarm that is stridently expressed towards it is wholly justified. If the misogyny that rap broadcasts reflect the broader cultural environment that we are socialised into, however, our reaction to it can be suspected of being selective at best and hypocritical at worst. As Tricia Rose (2008: 5) puts it by attacking easy mythologies that either accuse or excuse rap's violent misogyny, '[t]he excessive blame levelled at hip hop is astonishing in its refusal to consider the culpability of the larger social and political context'. This point is expressed with similar vigour by bell hooks (2006: 135) who sees the 'sexist, misogynist, patriarchal ways of thinking and behaving that are glorified in [...] rap' as a reflection of the prevailing values in our society, values created and sustained by white supremacist capitalist patriarchy'. Avid readers who are well-versed in Black feminist scholarship on rap, will quickly note that neither Rose (1990, 1994), nor hooks (2004) are strangers to critiques of ideologies, politics and practices of male domination – so their pointed comments carry special weight, as does the work of Kimberlé Crenshaw (1997) and Imani Perry (1995, 2004) who also warn against prejudicial oversimplifications of the violence in and complex gender and sexual politics of rap. This is not to hear the music by becoming blind to its misogynist narratives, but to stress that rap should be seen 'as a reflection of dominant values in our culture rather than as an aberrant pathological standpoint' (hooks, 2006: 135). Indeed, admitting this 'does not mean that a rigorous feminist critique and interrogation of the sexist and misogyny expressed in this music is not needed' (hooks, 2006: 135). Rather, rethinking misogyny in rap in this way simply advises that it ought to be placed within the social, cultural, political and economic environment that shapes it – namely, 'white supremacist capitalist patriarchy' that 'approves' and 'materially rewards' rappers' tales of misogyny and sexism (hooks, 2006: 143) by packaging and promoting violence against women as a branded commercial spectacle to be consumed as entertainment. What both Rose and hooks object to, therefore, is the discriminating and discriminatory demonisation of rap without being sensitive to the 'cultural crossing, mixings, and engagement of black youth culture with the values, attitudes, and concerns of the white majority' (hooks, 2006: 135), or attentive to how similar themes pass unnoticed in other forms of cultural expression that are granted poetic license, despite the fact that they, too may 'labor in the plantations of misogyny and sexism' (hooks, 2006: 143).

To illustrate this point, hooks observes how Jane Campion's art-house film *The Piano* is praised as 'an incredible film, a truly compelling love story' but '[n]o one speaking about this film mentions misogyny and sexism or white supremacist capitalist patriarchy' (hooks, 2006: 139). Set in the 'nineteenth-century world of the white invasion of New Zealand', as hooks (2006: 139) puts it, *The Piano* tells the story of Ada who is sold into marriage and expresses herself solely through playing the piano – having not spoken since childhood. After being refused her piano by her husband (Alisdair), due to lack of space in his patriarchal homestead, a neighbour (Baines) intervenes trading the piano for some of Alisdair's land; allowing Ada to reunite with her most precious possession, in exchange for molesting Ada while she plays. When Baines realises that it is not sexual assault that Ada visits him for but her chance to play the piano, he returns the piano and forces himself on her, cursing their arrangement for making Ada a 'whore' and him 'wretched'. Ada nevertheless returns to Baines, where she is spied on by Alisdair, who 'unable to win her back [...] expresses his rage, rooted in misogyny and sexism, by physically attacking her and chopping off her finger with an ax' (hooks, 2006: 140). Despite ample depictions of '[v]iolence against land, natives, and women', *The Piano's* high-art cinematography 'unlike [...] rap' is portrayed uncritically, as though [such imagery] is "natural" – the inevitable climax of conflicting passions' (hooks, 2006: 140). 'The outcome of this violence is all positive', hooks (2006: 140) notes, although the plotline 'betrays feminist visions of female actualization, celebrating and eroticizing male domination'. Such selectivity, inevitably begs the question of why it is acceptable for 'folks involved with high culture' to 'celebrate and condone the ideas and values upheld in this film', but decry 'those who celebrate and condone [...] rap' (hooks, 2006: 141). Blaming rap for the misogyny and sexism that passes unnoticed in highbrow art, therefore, makes attacks on rap vulnerable to accusations of double standards that falsely accuse rap, but also do violence to gendered liberation too – in ways that compromise the integrity of critique when it castigates violence against women in some forms of creative expression, but not others.

The *second* question that bedevils what Rose (2008) describes as 'the hip hop wars' surrounds the source of rap's misogyny. Having suggested above that rap shares its misogyny with art forms that are judged to be more elevated culturally, we now turn to the ideology that singles rap out as exceptionally misogynistic; through the demonisation of Black culture and young black men in particular who are labelled a 'cultural problem *as a group*' (Rose, 2008: 10; emphasis added) – in ways that would be unthinkable with reference to their white counterparts. As hooks (2006: 136) helpfully adds: 'black males, young and old, must be held politically accountable for their sexism. Yet this critique must always be contextualized or we risk making it appear that the problems of misogyny, sexism, and all the behaviors this thinking supports and condones, including rape, male violence against women, is a black male thing.' Exercising caution against interpreting misogyny (in rap) as 'merely a reflection of daily gender conflicts and negotiations among inner-city black youth' (Kelley, 1994: 221), the 'racist white

imagination' (hooks, 2006: 142) that sanctions such interpretations, therefore, cannot remain unnamed or critically unexamined. Situating misogyny
and sexism within specific forms of Black cultural expression, implicitly suggests that violence against women is inherent in and emanates from Black
culture as an exceptional, problematic and justifiably pathologised breeding
ground of gendered violence. While a 'very long and ignoble tradition of
sexism' (Kelley, 1994: 214) does exist in black vernacular culture, the same
applies to the dominant, Eurocentric, white mainstream culture that we are
educated and socialised into. As references to 'hoes' abound in rap music,
representations of women as 'bad', promiscuous 'whores' who dishonour
themselves by violating patriarchal idea(l)s of chastity and marital bond-
age, are also prevalent in the most revered and sacred repositories of mainstream Western culture. Couched in variations of the 'Madonna-Whore
Dichotomy' (Kahalon et al., 2019), the female body in the Western cultural
canon is variously viewed as dangerous, unclean and a source of potential
contamination in moralistic language that drips with sexualised violence
against women. In Chapter 17 of the *Book of Revelation*, Babylon is sym-
bolised as a 'great whore' who will eventually be made 'desolate and naked',
her 'flesh' 'devoured' and 'burn[t] up with fire'. Sigmund Freud's (1933) classic lectures on psychoanalysis depict women as anatomically inferior, envi-
ous and resentful; ostensibly suffering from penis envy. Cesare Lombroso's
(1958) positivist criminology attributed physical and moral 'anomalies' to
female offenders, describing prostitutes as a criminal category that possesses degenerate characteristics. Ovid's *Metamorphoses* is rife with rape
scenes, the most famous of which being the Greek myth of Europa's rape
by Zeus – which is deemed so central a symbol of European culture as to
name an entire continent (Europe) after it. Friedrich Nietzsche's *Thus Spoke
Zarathustra* dutifully reminds readers: 'You are going to women? Do not
forget the whip!' (Burgard, 1994: 4) and many more examples of violent
misogyny could be plucked from the pantheon of Western culture. Yet, even
when such texts are contextualised or criticised, they are hardly dismissed
as sources of cultural pathology or outright misogyny. Instead, they feature as classic works of religious instruction, psychoanalytical scholarship,
criminological history, literary appreciation and philosophical meditation.

The *third* question that brings us closer to the source of the selective blame
that is heaped on rap as a cesspool of sexist misogyny, invites us to think
about the very worldview that sets attacks on rap in motion. This worldview and logic have a name: racism, but it remains conspicuously absent
from such debates – despite its ominous presence as the dominant way of
seeing the world from the perspective and social location of the white mainstream; white feminism included. Contrary to popular (mis)conceptions of
racism that treat it as 'a mental quirk', 'a psychological flaw' (Fanon, 1967:
88), an individual attribute or as mere behaviour, racism is approached
here as 'a structure not an event' (Wolfe, 2006: 390). Racism is *systemic*,
structural, institutional(ised). It is not *episodic*, accidental or the outcome

of a few unfortunate, isolated incidents that suddenly erupt out of nowhere. Much like sexism, racism should be understood as the very socio-cultural and political context that shapes and defines social life. Rather than a deviation from such a context, racism is an exclusionary ideology, a structural feature and an active ingredient of a social system of racialised hierarchy that creates institutional patterns, organisations, structures, cultures and politics of social injustice and social exclusion. Racism, therefore, is not simply what somebody thinks about or does to someone who is perceived, defined, classified and understood – primarily if not exclusively – as a member of a particular (minority) racial or ethnic group. It is a socio-cultural, political, institutional mentality, worldview and ideology which assigns a negative value to biological and cultural differences that are perceived as alien, incomprehensible, and inadmissible to a (majority) white society and its social institutions.

Acknowledging racism as the perspective and the social location from which critiques on rap are mounted, is therefore essential for a sober appraisal of the stigmatisation that rap suffers. Yet, even progressive socio-political movements like feminism, or rather its 'white' variant, fail to recognise their complicity in the racist logic(s) that essentialise misogyny by disproportionately blaming it on Black forms of cultural expression. Charging white feminism with racism might sound unfair, but it is impossible to ignore a blind spot that chips away at the movement's integrity as a scholarly perspective and a radical political force. Just as our appreciation of rap music should not silence concerns about its misogyny, our commitment to feminist politics should not obscure the whiteness that sneaks into its worldview. Pretending that feminism doesn't construct itself by default as normatively and universally 'white', is to ignore and dismiss a rich Black feminist tradition that emerged as a response to feminist politics that assume that 'all the women are white' or that 'all the Blacks are men' (Hull et al., 1982), as the title of a Black feminist classic has it[1]. As Audre Lorde observes, '[u]nchallenged, racism ultimately will be the death of the women's movement in England, just as it threatens to become the death of any women's movement in those developed countries where it is not addressed' (Parmar and Kay, 1988: 125). Exaggerated though such a warning may sound, racism has nevertheless been endemic in white feminism, permeating foundational texts of the movement. Consider Mary Wollstonecraft's (1985: 310–311) *Vindication of the Rights of Woman*, which depicted enslaved Black women as showing an 'immoderate fondness for dress, for pleasure, and for sway', dismissing these as 'the passions of savages; the passions that occupy those uncivilised human beings who have not yet extended the dominion of mind'. Think also about how later modern classics like Shulamith Firestone's *The Dialectic of Sex* 'addres[s] black women's issues in a single chapter, and everywhere else in the book, 'woman' – a universal and unmodified noun – does not mean *them*' (Spillers, 2003: 159). Or think about how standard critiques of rape and sexualised male violence, like Susan Brownmiller's *Against our Will*, are 'so intent on pursuing the black-man-as rapist theme that [...] black women's sexual experience, static and reified [...] strike the reader as a rather perverse and exotic exercise' (Spillers, 2003: 160). These selective passages do not encompass the entire canon of white feminist literature, nor do they pretend to offer an overview of white feminism's racism. Rather, they are mentioned here as a confrontation with white feminist critiques of rap's misogyny that remain oblivious to their own racism. Were this not so, there would not be an entire tradition of Black women's thought that rejects the term 'feminism' to describe its gender politics; opting instead for the word 'womanism'; as a word that 'encompasses 'feminist' [...] but also means *instinctively* pro-woman' with 'blackness [being] implicit in the term' (Walker, 1980: 100). 'An advantage of using "womanist"', Walker (1980: 100) explains, 'is that, because it is from my own culture, I needn't preface it with the word "Black" (an awkward necessity and a problem I have with the word "feminist"), since blackness is implicit in the term; just as for white women there is apparently no felt need to preface "feminist" with the word "white" since the word "feminist" is accepted as coming out of white women's culture'[2]. White feminism's reluctance to interrogate the ways in which its whiteness – as an invisibilised power relation – distorts its agenda for women's liberation, is especially audible in the way it overlooks Black women's agency –including Black women rappers – when misogyny in rap is discussed. In so doing, a long history of 'talkin' up to the white woman' (Moreton-Robinson, 2020) is ignored – as is the contribution of 'hip-hop' feminism (Morgan, 1999; David, 2007; Peoples, 2008) by Black women rappers who 'wreck' (Pough, 2004) misogynistic representations of Black women within rap. While Black women rappers make room for a progressive feminist 'stage' (Durham *et al.*, 2013) that openly challenges misogyny, white feminist critique assumes that 'images of Black women as sexually available hoochies' (Collins, 2000: 85) are not sufficiently resisted by their non-white 'sisters'.

Isn't it violent?

Violence has long been a central theme in the aesthetic vocabulary of some rap subgenres, especially 1990s 'gangsta rap' and its offshoots; including drill music today (Fatsis, 2019b; Ilan, 2020). Such graphic imagery depicts 'criminal' lifestyles, where references to firearms, knives, drugs and gang violence are common – as are lurid tales of fictional larger-than-life personas who tell their story in the first person and pose as unabashedly violent. (Mis)taken for literal threats of violence rather than confrontational boasts that reflect the artistic conventions of the genre, rap features prominently on the law enforcement radar and is frequently put 'on trial' (Nielson and Dennis, 2019) as evidence of criminal wrongdoing. As such, rap lyrics are translated into autobiographical confessions of already committed offences, or expressions of intent or motive for offences to be committed – rather than as first-person narratives that may be partly or purely performative, fictional, hyperbolic or fabricated even; as is the case with many other music lyrics or literary works (Bramwell, 2018: 484; Fatsis, 2019b: 1301; Ilan, 2020: 2, 3, 6, 13, 16; Stuart, 2020: 195). Acknowledging the artistic nature of violent rap lyrics does not justify, excuse, or encourage its enjoyment with relish – nor does it justify the hostile, discriminatory, illiberal and unjust way(s) in which it is criminalised, policed against and prosecuted through 'street illiterate', 'inaccurate' and ultimately 'counterproductive' tactics (Ilan, 2020). It simply offers a contextual reading of violence in rap, by urging that we focus on *how* it is violent. Is violence in rap real or performative? Is it an expression of 'criminal' intent or a bid for commercial success? Does rap celebrate violence or does it comment on it? These questions are taken up in turn, to do justice to accusations of violence in rap that tell us more about the discriminatory logic, mission and function of criminal legal institutions and their racial politics of law and order (Fatsis, 2021a) than they do about rap.

Starting with the nature of violence in rap, the genre's cast of 'gangstas', 'thugs' and 'hustlas' are examples of 'badman' archetypes that have a long pedigree in 'black vernacular folklore' (Kelley, 1994: 191) featuring outlaw legends like Stagolee and MacDaddy who fearlessly defy societal norms with casual bravado (Toop, 2000: 34; Quinn, 2005; Gunter, 2008; Nielson and Dennis, 2019). The adoption of similar violent personas in rap, therefore, are a continuation of such literary conventions rather than evidence of involvement in violent acts (Krims, 2000). As Stoia et al. (2018: 330) argue 'fictionalized accounts of violence form the stock-in-trade of rap and should not be interpreted literally'. Treating them as literal truth, means interpreting art in a legalistic context where they are deemed 'true threats' and prosecuted as such. Rapping about a crime – even alluding to a real crime – cannot be interpreted as equivalent to an admission made by an actual person (rather than a character or persona) made *outside* the artistic context of a musical composition. Such a suggestion is often accused of placing rap lyrics beyond the reach of forensic scrutiny or legal debate, potentially allowing miscreants to safely record their wrongdoings as long as they write about them in rap verse. Yet, the problem with including first person narratives in rhyme form as evidence is that it is applied selectively to rap music and its various subgenres; thereby having a prejudicial impact on court proceedings due to stereotypical associations between drill and crime, crime and gang membership, and indeed Black culture and criminality (see, e.g. Gilroy, 1987; Fischoff, 1999; Fried, 1999; Dennis, 2007; Kubrin and Nielson, 2014; Young Review, 2014; Lammy Review, 2017; Owusu-Bempah, 2017, 2020; Dunbar and Kubrin, 2018; Williams and Clarke, 2018; Fatsis, 2019a, 2019b; Phillips *et al.*, 2020; Paul, 2021). As Nielson and Dennis (2019: 114) remind us '[r]ap is not the only art to trade in outlaw [...] narratives', nor is it 'the only art form to draw from real life for its creations'. Any close 'reading' of country music lyrics (Fried, 1999), 17th century English folk music (Thompson, 1992), opera librettos (Hartford, 2016), or any music genre that 'levers people's wild side over their inhibitions' (Toop, 2000: 166) would suffice to attest to that fact. Yet rap is 'the only form of artistic expression to be mischaracterized as pure autobiography [or] real world documentary' (Nielson and Dennis, 2019: 114).

To illustrate that with an example, Stormzy – who poses as a 'WickedSkengman' (meaning 'wicked gunman' or 'wicked knifeman') on 'WickedSkengman 5' – raps: 'My n****z they don't talk, they shoot'. Such references to 'shooting' rather than 'talking' could be taken literally. Doing so, however, would distort the meaning and violate the context of this verse by conflating the narrator of the lyrics with the rapper, while also ignoring the use of inversion in rap lyrics where rhymes mean the opposite of what they say. Drawing on such a verse as evidence of involvement in violent crime, would therefore mean labelling, accusing and pursuing Stormzy as someone whose career ostensibly revolves around shooting rather than rapping. Yet, this is the same artist who has won Album of the Year at the 2018 Brit Awards and established a Cambridge University scholarship programme. He is therefore not the 'WickedSkengman' that his rapped first-person narrative describes. Rather, Stormzy is using poetic license to adopt a 'badman' persona to excite fans following long-established genre norms.

According to such norms, violent content is actually expected as a lyrical motif within rap – whose connections to literal truth are rhetorical. These claims and performances are part of an economy of authenticity by which artists compete for relevance and popularity through telling violent stories, not unlike Hollywood gangster films or popular video games. In fact, much of the appeal of commercial, mainstream rap depends on consciously exploiting stereotypes of violence, gangsterism and 'ghetto life' as a sought-after commodity to be consumed online by followers whose clicks, views, likes and shares can and *do* yield material rewards (Stuart, 2020). Rather than offering a simple 'authentic' voice, rappers are highly attuned to the commercial relations of their work. They deploy themes of violence and crime that they know to be very marketable. A central impetus and theme of the music is the desire to become a successful rapper to escape poverty and the violence is part of the genre's conventions and part of its commercial appeal too. A broader reading of the genre, therefore, reveals deeply ambiguous relationships to violence that cannot be simply described as 'glorifying' them – contrary to what criminal (in)justice institutions and their personnel erroneously and misleadingly contend (Fatsis, 2019b; Nielson and Dennis, 2019: 157, 319; Ilan, 2020), drawing on questionable expertise (Lutes *et al.*, 2019; Lerner and Kubrin, 2021; Paul, 2021: 41; Ward and Fouladvand, 2021).

In addition to performative dimension of violence in rap, the reality of violence that rappers are often accused of glamourising is also misunderstood as being *dictated* by rappers, rather than *narrated* by them. As a result, shocked reactions to violent rap lyrics focus on the lyrics but overlook the realities they portray. '[S]tructural forms of deep racism, corporate influences, and the long-term effects of economic, social and political disempowerment', therefore, become separated from 'rappers' alienated angry stories about life in the ghetto' and 'seen as "proof" that black behaviour creates ghetto conditions' (Rose, 2008: 5) – making 'decades of urban racial discrimination (the reason black ghettos exist in the first place), in every significant area – housing, education, jobs, social services – in every city with a significant black population, [...] disappear from view' (Rose, 2008: 5). Following such a logic, rapping about violence is blamed for causing violence rather than as being read as social commentary that exposes the violence that prevails in neighbourhoods that racist social policy shapes into 'zones of racial enclosure characterised by extreme deprivation and regular violence' (Hartman, 2021: 94). To make matters worse, accusing violent lyrics for the violence they broadcast and comment on, doesn't just direct our attention away from how 'extremity' and '[v]iolation teaches violence' (Jordan, 1995: 180). It also denies rappers the possibility of expressing negative angry emotions to purge them away, by treating every violent verse as proof of 'criminality' – rather than as an examples of purification through creative expression, not unlike the function of catharsis in tragedy that Aristotle's *Poetics* defends as socially beneficial (Nicholl, 1980: 142). Seen this way, violent lyrics become an outlet for artistic production that makes room for young people to come to voice, articulate their thoughts, explore their emotions and respond to their social environment by translating their anger, bitterness and frustration into rap lyrics, instead of picking up a knife or a gun (Toop, 2000: 166, 169–170; Nielson and Dennis, 2019: 30). Such an approach to violent rap lyrics, however, is often accused of excusing violence and dismissed as an ostentatious display of permissiveness that is out of touch with empirical reality. Yet, such an accusation is itself to blame for confusing *rationalising* violence with *contextualising* it, while also neglecting forms of structural and state violence as the reality that breeds violence in the first place (Fatsis, 2019b: 1304–1305; Lynes *et al.*, 2020).

Having surveyed accusations of sexual and 'criminal' violence in rap should have hitherto encouraged us to resist a '"blame and explain" festival' where '[o]ne side attacks and blames, and the other side explains' (Rose, 2008: 129). Yet, the temptation of taking sides often overrides the necessity of flipping the script through language and politics that should refuse to discuss misogyny and violence in rap – without attending to the complex and nuanced socio-cultural and political considerations that shape such controversies. As Tricia Rose (2008: 27) wisely counsels, it is possible – as it is necessary – to find ways to 'critique hip hop without bashing the entire genre', just as there are ways of 'support[ing]' it without nourishing sexist, homophobic, or racist ideas'. Such a shift in our thinking, however, requires an attitude towards gender, racial and criminal justice that turns its critical attention to the dominant social order and the political systems that uphold it by and through divisions of both gender and 'race'. Racialised as 'white' and gendered as male, this is the very racist, patriarchal order that criminal justice institutions serve, protect and maintain. Yet, little of the critical fire that rap draws is directed at the way our social world is put together through interlocking systems of oppression that Black feminist intellectuals took pains to lay bare (see, e.g. Hull *et al.*, 1982: 13–22). With Black radical feminist thought as our guide, questions of misogyny and violence inevitably become questions of political violence. If we are to understand anything about the law and order politics that (in)forms criminal justice system definitions of who and what is 'criminal', we also ought to understand something about the ideological nature of state violence as patriarchal and racist (Wynter, 2003). And to understand state violence, we need to understand that state formation itself is violent, depending as it does on an extractive and repressive logic that is imposed and therefore coercive by its very nature (Tilly, 1985, 1992; Robinson, 2016). And this extractive and repressive logic is disproportionately exercised on those who are gendered and racialised as subordinate and *un*belonging to the dominant patriarchal and racial order. Given the deep historical roots of patriarchy and racism as ideologies of political power that have erected social and cultural institutions that we are born into, misogyny and violence become easier to detect and decry in forms of Black popular culture – like rap – than they are to blame on the patriarchal violence that pervades political economic and cultural systems of oppression every day. Developing such new thinking habits, however, involves readjusting our worldview to understand that the realities that our words describe are dictated by the vocabulary of an unequal social order where misogyny and violence become crimes only if they are identified as what Saidiya Hartman (2021: 220) calls 'status offense[s]'; acts that are 'deemed illegal only for a particular group of persons', but not others. As this chapter has attempted to reveal, the punitive language with which rap is perceived as exceptionally misogynistic and violent is shaped by a moral vocabulary that uses social status to determine whether what people are and do or whether they should be punished for the same activities that are rarely criminalised in the social and political lives of others. Through such thinking, 'crime' becomes a matter of *being* rather than *doing* to denote who belongs and who doesn't. Accusations of misogyny and violence, therefore, serve as excuses that the white mainstream invents to police blackness through music (Fatsis, 2021b). Were this not so, Black music genres like rap would not be stereotypically identified with misogyny and violence – nor would 'criminality [be] tethered ineradicably to blackness' (Hartman, 2021: 243). Critics of misogyny and violence – however sincere they may wish to be – may need to look elsewhere for the crimes that Black music genres take the rap for.

Notes

1 For a masterly discussion of how blackness is theorised, constructed and fictionalised as property, object or what she calls a 'surrogate' through which the white imagination asserts itself, see Morrison (1993: 26).

2 For further discussion on womanism, see Ogunyemi (1985), Cannon (1988), Smitherman (1996), Hill Collins (1998) and Hudson-Weems (1998).

References

Bramwell, R. (2018) "Freedom within Bars: Maximum Security Prisoners' Negotiations of Identity through Rap". *Identities*, 25(4): 475–492.

Burgard, P.J. (1994) *Nietzsche and the Feminine*. London: University Press of Virginia.

Cannon, K.G. (1988) *Black Womanist Ethics*. Atlanta: Scholars Press.

Collins, P.H. (1998) *Fighting Words: Black Women and the Search for Justice*. Minneapolis: University of Minnesota Press.

Collins, P.H. (2000) *Black Feminist Thought: Knowledge, Consciousness and the Politics of Empowerment*. London: Routledge.

Crenshaw, K.W. (1997) "Beyond Racism and Misogyny: Black Feminism and 2 Live Crew". In: Meyers, D.T. (ed.) *Feminist Social Thought: A Reader*. London: Routledge, pp. 245–263.

David, M. (2007) "More than Baby Mamas: Black Mothers and Hip-Hop Feminism". In Pough, G.D. *et al.* (eds.) *Home Girls Make Some Noise: Hip Hop Feminism Anthology*. Mira Loma: Parker Publishing, pp. 345–367.

Dennis, A.L. (2007) "Poetic (In)Justice? Rap Music Lyrics as Art, Life, and Criminal Evidence". *The Columbia Journal of Law and the Arts*, 31: 1–41.

Dunbar, A. and Kubrin, C.E. (2018) "Imagining Violent Criminals: An Experimental Investigation of Music Stereotypes and Character Judgments". *Journal of Experimental Criminology*, 14(4): 507–528.

Durham, A., Cooper, B.C. and Morris, S.M. (2013) "The Stage Hip-Hop Feminism Built: A New Directions Essay". *Signs*, 38(3): 721–737.

Fanon, F. (1967) *Toward the African Revolution: Political Essays*. New York: Grove Press.

Fatsis, L. (2019a) "Grime: Criminal Subculture or Public Counterculture? A Critical Investigation into the Criminalization of Black Musical Subcultures in the UK". *Crime Media Culture*, 15(3), 447–461.

Fatsis, L. (2019b) "Policing the Beats: The Criminalisation of UK Drill and Grime Music by the London Metropolitan Police". *The Sociological Review*, 67(6): 1300–1316.

Fatsis, L. (2021a) "Policing the Union's Black: The Racial Politics of Law and Order in Contemporary Britain". In: Gordon, F. and Newman, D. (eds.) *Leading Works in Law and Social Justice*. London: Routledge, pp. 137–150.

Fatsis, L. (2021b) "Sounds Dangerous: Black Music Subcultures as Victims of State Regulation and Social Control". In: Peršak, N. and Di Ronco, A. (eds.) *Harm and Disorder in the Urban Space: Social Control, Sense and Sensibility*. London: Routledge, pp. 30–51.

Fischoff, S.P. (1999) "Gangsta' Rap and a Murder in Bakersfield". *Journal of Applied Social Psychology*, 29(4): 795–805.

Freud, S. (1933) *New Introductory Lectures on Psychoanalysis*. New York: Norton & Co.

Fried, C.B. (1999) "Who's Afraid of Rap: Differential Reactions to Music Lyrics". *Journal of Applied Social Psychology*, 29(4): 705–721.

Gilroy, P. (1987) "The Myth of Black Criminality". In: Scraton, P. (ed.) *Law, Order and the Authoritarian State: Readings in Critical Criminology*. London: Open University Press, pp. 47–56.

Guevara, N. (1996) "Women Writin' Rappin' Breakin'". In: Perskin, W.E. (ed.) *Droppin' Science: Critical Essays on Rap Music and Hip Hop Culture*. Philadelphia: Temple University Press, pp. 49–62.

Gunter, A. (2008) "Growing Up Bad: Black Youth 'Road' Culture and Badness in an East London Neighbourhood". *Crime Media Culture,* 4(3): 349–365.

Hartford, K.L. (2016) "Beyond the Trigger Warning: Teaching Operas that Depict Sexual Violence". *Journal of Music History Pedagogy,* 7(1): 19–34.

Hartman, S. (2021) *Wayward Lives, Beautiful Experiments.* London: Serpent's Tail.

hooks, b. (2004) *We Real Cool: Black Men and Masculinity.* London: Routledge.

hooks, b. (2006) *Outlaw Culture: Resisting Representations.* London: Routledge.

Hudson-Weems, C. (1998) "Africana Womanism". In: Nnaemeka, O. (ed.) *Sisterhood, Feminisms, and Power: From Africa to the Diaspora.* Trenton, NJ: Africa World Press, pp. 149–162.

Hull, A.G.T., Bell-Scott, P. and Smith, B. (1982) *All the Women Are White, All the Blacks Are Men, but Some of Us Are Brave.* New York: The Feminist Press.

Ilan, J. (2020) "Digital Street Culture Decoded: Why Criminalizing Drill Music Is Street Illiterate and Counterproductive". *The British Journal of Criminology,* 60(4), 994–1013.

Jordan, J. (1995) *Civil Wars.* New York: Simon and Schuster, p. 180.

Kahalon, R. *et al.* (2019) "The Madonna-Whore Dichotomy Is Associated with Patriarchy Endorsement: Evidence from Israel, the United States, and Germany". *Psychology of Women Quarterly,* 43(3): 348–367.

Kelley, R.D.G. (1994) *Race Rebels: Culture, Politics and the Black Working Class.* New York: Free Press.

Keyes, C.L. (1993) "'We're More than a Novelty, Boys': Strategies of Female Rappers in the Rap Music Tradition". In: Radner, J.N. (ed.) *Feminist Messages: Coding in Women's Folk Culture.* Urbana: University of Illinois Press, pp. 203–319.

Krims, A. (2000) *Rap Music and the Poetics of Identity.* Cambridge: Cambridge University Press.

Kubrin, C.E. (2005) "Gangstas, Thugs, and Hustlas: Identity and the Code of the Street in Rap Music". *Social Problems,* 52(3), 360–378.

Kubrin, C.E. and Nielson, E. (2014) "Rap on Trial". *Race and Justice,* 4(3), 185–211.

Lammy Review (2017) "An Independent Review of the Treatment of and Outcomes for Black, Asian and Minority Ethnic individuals in the Criminal Justice System". Available at: https://www.gov.uk/government/uploads/system/uploads/attachment_data/file/643001/lammy-review-final-report.pdf [Accessed 28 August, 2021].

Lerner, J.I. and Kubrin, C.E. (2021) "Rap on Trial: A Legal Guide for Attorneys". *UC Irvine School of Law Research Paper,* No. 2021-35.

Lombroso, C. (1958). *The Female Offender.* New York: Philosophical Library.

Lutes, E., Purdon, J. and Fradella, H.F. (2019) "When Music Takes the Stand: A Content Analysis of How Courts Use and Misuse Rap Lyrics in Criminal Cases". *American Journal of Criminal Law,* 46(1): 77–132.

Lynes, A., Kelly, C. and Kelly, E. (2020) "Thug Life: Drill Music as a Periscope into Urban Violence in the Consumer Age". *The British Journal of Criminology* 60(5): 1201–1219.

Moreton-Robinson, A. (2020) *Talkin' Up to the White Woman: Indigenous Women and Feminism.* St. Lucia: UQP.

Morgan, J. (1999) *When Chickenheads Come Home to Roost: A Hip-Hop Feminist Breaks It Down.* New York: Simon & Schuster.

Morrison. T. (1993) *Playing in the Dark: Whiteness and the Literary Imagination.* New York: Vintage.

Nicholl, C. (1980) *The Chemical Theatre.* London: Routledge.

Nielson, E. and Dennis, A.L. (2019) *Rap on Trial Race, Lyrics, and Guilt in America*. New York: New Press.

Ogunyemi, C.O. (1985) "Womanism: The Dynamics of the Contemporary Black Female Novel in English". *Signs*, 11(1): 63–80.

Owusu-Bempah, A. (2017) "Race and Policing in Historical Context: Dehumanization and the Policing of Black People in the 21st Century". *Theoretical Criminology*, 21(1): 23–34.

Owusu-Bempah, A. (2020) "Part of Art or Part of Life? Rap Lyrics in Criminal Trials". *LSE Blogs*. Available at: https://blogs.lse.ac.uk/politicsandpolicy/rap-lyrics-in-criminal-trials/ [Accessed 28 August 2021].

Parmar, P. and Kay. J. (1988) "Frontiers. Pratibha Parmar and Jackie Kay Interview Audre Lorde Nielson and Dennis, 2019: 30". In: Grewal, S. (ed.) *Charting the Journey: Writings by Black and Third World Women*. London: Sheba, pp. 121–131.

Paul, S. (2021) *Tackling Racial Injustice: Children and the Youth Justice System: A Report by JUSTICE*. London: Justice.

Peoples, W.A. (2008) "'Under Construction': Identifying Foundations of Hip-Hop Feminism and Exploring Bridges between Black Second-Wave and Hip-Hop Feminisms". *Meridians* 8(1): 19–52.

Perry, I. (1995) "It's My Thang and I'll Swing It the Way That I Feel!". In: Dines, G. and Humez, J. (eds.) *Gender, Race and Class in Media*. Thousand Oaks: Sage, pp. 524–530.

Perry, I. (2004) *Prophets of the Hood: Politics and Poetics in Hip Hop*. Durham: Duke University Press.

Phillips, C., Earle, R., Parmar, A. *et al.* (2020) "Dear British Criminology: Where Has All the Race and Racism Gone?" *Theoretical Criminology*, 24(3): 427–446.

Pough, G.D. (2004) *Check It While I Wreck It: Black Womanhood, Hip-Hop Culture, and the Public Sphere*. Boston: Northeastern University Press.

Quinn, E. (2005) *Nuthin' But a G Thang: The Culture and Commerce of Gangsta Rap*. New York: Columbia University Press.

Robinson, C.J. (2016) *The Terms of Order: Political Science and the Myth of Leadership*. Chapel Hill: The University of North Carolina Press.

Rose, T. (1990) "Never Trust A Big Butt and A Smile". *Camera Obscura*, 23, 108–131.

Rose, T. (1994) *Black Noise: Rap Music and Black Culture in Contemporary America*. Hanover: Wesleyan University Press.

Rose, T. (2008) *The Hip Hop Wars: What We Talk about When We Talk about Hip Hop–and Why It Matters*. New York: Basic Books.

Smitherman, G. (1996) "A Womanist Looks at the Million Man March". In: Madhubuti, H.R. and Karenga, M. (eds) *Million Man March/Day of Absence*, Chicago: Third World Press, pp. 104–107.

Spillers, H. (2003) *Black, White, and in Color: Essays on American Literature and Culture*. London: The University of Chicago Press.

Stoia, N., Adams, K. and Drakulich, K. (2018) "Rap Lyrics as Evidence: What Can Music Theory Tell Us?" *Race and Justice* 2018, 8(4): 330–365.

Stuart, F. (2020) *Ballad of the Bullet: Gangs, Drill Music and the Power of Online Infamy*. Princeton: Princeton University Press.

Thompson, E.P. (1992) "Rough Music Reconsidered". *Folklore* 103(1): 3–26.

Tilly, C. (1985) "War Making and State Making as Organized Crime". In: Evans, P., Rueschemeyer, D. and Skocpol, T. (eds.) *Bringing the State Back In*. Cambridge: Cambridge University Press, pp. 170–186.

Tilly, C. (1992) *Coercion, Capital, and European States AD 900–1992*. Cambridge: Blackwell.

Toop, D. (2000) *Rap Attack #3: African Rap to Global Hip Hop*. London: Serpent's Tail.

Walker, A. (1980) "Coming Apart". In: Lederer, L. (ed.) *Take Back the Night: Women on Pornography*. New York: William Morrow and Company, pp. 95–104.

Ward, T. and Fouladvand, S. (2021) "Bodies of Knowledge and Robes of Expertise: Expert Evidence about Drugs, Gangs and Human Trafficking". *Criminal Law Review*, 6: 442–460.

Williams, P. and Clarke, B. (2018) "The Black Criminal Other as an Object of Social Control". *Social Sciences*, 7(234): 1–14.

Wolfe, P. (2006) "Settler Colonialism and the Elimination of the Native". *Journal of Genocide Research*, 8(4): 387–409.

Wollstonecraft, M. (1985) *Vindication of the Rights of Women*. Harmondsworth: Penguin.

Wynter, S. (2003) "Unsettling the Coloniality of Being/Power/Truth/Freedom: Towards the Human, After Man, Its Overrepresentation–An Argument". *CR: The New Centennial Review* 3(3): 257–337.

Young Review (2014) "Improving Outcomes for Young Black and/or Muslim Men in the Criminal Justice System". Available at: http://www.youngreview.org.uk/sites/default/files/clinks_young-review_report_dec2014.pdf [Accessed 28 August 2021].

7 Music

Human Rights and Harms

Eleanor Peters

Introduction

Criminology covers a large number of issues, but this chapter will bring together two areas that have been relatively under-explored in the discipline, music and human rights. The analysis of human rights was given considerable criminological emphasis by Stan Cohen in his work in the 1990s identifying the illegitimacy of states that violate their citizens' rights and outlining the many forms of denial that governments utilise in the face of human right abuses (Cohen, 1985, 1993). As Green and Ward (2000) identify, there are two approaches to understanding human rights[1]; one is the 'torture' paradigm where there is common agreement about evils that can never be acceptable or justified, while the other approach looks at the importance of personal well-being, such as health and access to education. Criminology is a rare academic discipline because its object of study is imposed and defined by the state; however, in a bid to widen definitions of crime to include damage and injury that may not necessarily be against the law, many critical criminologists have called for an understanding of issues wider than that of state defined crime towards that of harms; an approach that lends itself well to the study of violations of human rights[2].

Human rights discourses incorporate issues of morality, politics, equality, and individual and collective social justice. Criminologists, particularly those from a critical criminological position, may well consider the theory of natural law to explain that just because something may be legal, it does not necessarily mean that it is morally fair, as the historical example of apartheid in South Africa validates. In this vein, modern human rights theorists tend to conceptualise rights as social constructions, driven as much by politics as anything else (Freeman, 2017). Tasioulas (2013) suggests that human rights may be considered as moral standards to which a variety of legal and political instruments profess to give expression and force, but critical criminologists and zemiologists would consider there are limitations to consideration of rights via legalistic decrees.

DOI: 10.4324/9781003186410-7

Using human rights (and harms) to analyse music and sound

Sound can be perceived as pleasurable or unpleasant, although the boundary that separates music and noise can subjective. Noise, such as the sounds of heavy traffic, is usually considered disagreeable sounds while music is considered melodious (Idrobo-Ávila et al., 2018). Music may be regarded as affirmative sound whereas noise is unpleasant and unwanted (Thompson, 2014). Music is a socially defined arrangement of sounds construed and constructed by performers and listeners, and different types of music maintain their own aesthetic through social and cultural construction (Washburne and Derno, 2004) whereby music is used to satisfy a need for group identity because as Biancorosso (2004, p. 191) states 'taste in music thus – mirrors-and validates-the existing social order'. Bourdieu (2010) argued that taste is a marker of social class as those with a high social standing have inherited cultural capital. High culture encompasses the cultural objects of aesthetic value, which a society collectively holds in elevated esteem, and this is reflected in what a society deems as exemplary art, for example classical rather than popular music (Kotarba, 2009).

However, music has many functions within society. Thompson (1997, p. vi) describes music as the 'poetics of transgression', as unconventional and experimental music has potential to shock and unnerve – qualities which give it power. As DeNora (2004) points out, some music is controlled and regulated because of how dangerous it might be. When powerful agents of control[3] define the meanings of cultural products, this can result in diminished freedoms through laws that restrain and regulate popular culture (DeNora, 2010).

This chapter will consider human rights approaches as outlined above, analysing the abuse of music by the state in the form of torture 'lite' and examining the suppression and regulation of so-called dangerous sounds and musicians. The state can be in the absurd position of having the power to define and then control some music as being obscene or dangerous or deviant, while employing it for their own punishing objectives. Human rights encompass issues of morality, politics, equality, and individual and collective social justice. This chapter focuses on how music can be understood as violating human rights and causing damage in terms of tangible harm, for example, direct violence such as torture and physical and psychological harm. Additionally, there is symbolic violence in suppressing culture and erosion of freedom of expression through state and corporate repression of music and musicians (Salmi, 2004).

Tangible violence: Torture

Renewed interest in music as an element of modern torture techniques resulted from reports which emerged from Abu Graib prison and Guantanamo Bay concerning the mistreatment of detainees by US forces following the 11 September 2001 attacks in New York and Washington

(Amnesty International, 2021; Smeulers and Niekerk, 2009). Music (and sound) was used alongside a range of so-called 'torture-lite' approaches, known euphemistically as enhanced interrogation. Techniques, such as waterboarding which makes the victim feel as if they are drowning, were designed to cause psychological stress but not leave physical signs of harm (Cusick, 2006). Loud music and sounds were used alongside sensory deprivation, such as hooding to cause sleep deprivation and disorientation. Binyam Mohamed, held by the US authorities as a suspected Taliban fighter, described being tortured in Guantanamo Bay; 'it was pitch black... there was loud [rap] music, Eminem's Slim Shady and Dr. Dre for 20 days' (Swash, 2008). Shafiq Rasul, one of the Tipton 3[4] reported being chained in a stress position[5] to the floor of a minuscule booth which was extremely dark except for regular blinding flashes of a strobe light, with air-conditioning on so high that it was almost freezing. Additionally, there was loud, menacing heavy metal music being played. Rasul said; 'even if you were shouting, the music was too loud – nobody would be able to hear you. You're there for hours and hours, and they're constantly playing the same music. All that builds up. You start hallucinating' (Piesner, 2006).

Music that in other contexts might be associated with leisure and enjoyment has now become a tool of torment. Music, or indeed any noise, can be a source of pain and the result of excessive sound can result in slower thinking, neurosis, dyspnoea, heart palpitations and ectopic beats, elevated blood pressure, and speech problems (Attali, 1984). Any repetitious noise can be used for harm but in cases such as Guantanamo Bay, the choice of music – usually heavy metal and rap – was dissonant and alien to most of those who were detained (Borger, 2003). For example, during interrogations of Iraqi fighters, American interrogators played the song *Enter Sandman* by the heavy metal group Metallica, which they apparently found to be effective as an interrogation tool (Smyczek, 2005). There are clear ideological reasons for choosing to use a genre such as heavy metal; it is frequently disliked by the majority (Bryson, 1996) and perceived as loud and angry outsider music (Gilman, 2010). This perception is given added kudos by some of those who produce it[6], such as the lead singer of the aforementioned Metallica. When asked about his music being torture, James Hetfield said; 'we've been punishing our parents, our wives, our loved ones with this music for ever. Why should the Iraqis be any different?' (Stafford Smith, 2008). Bassist Steve Benton of Drowning Pool, a group whose song *Bodies* was used in interrogations said;

> People assume we should be offended that somebody in the military thinks our song is annoying enough that played over and over it can psychologically break someone down. I take it as an honor to think that perhaps our song could be used to quell another 9/11 attack or something like that.
>
> (Keating, 2008)

The band appear in the film *Songs of War* (2012), where they acknowledge awareness of soldiers (mis)using their music in Iraq. The film follows the journey taken by composer Christopher Cerf when he discovers, to his dismay, that one of his compositions, the theme from the children's television programme *Sesame Street* was used by US intelligence services to torture detainees. In the film, he meets soldiers and ex-prisoners who discuss their experiences of music as torture, including an interview with members of Drowning Pool, who avoid Cerf's questions their music being used as an interrogation tool, instead joking about how their music could be perceived as torture for people who don't enjoy metal, in a similar manner to that of Hetfield, from Metallica.

There are those who might also think this amusing, because everyone 'knows' listening to heavy metal is torture, although there are other examples of certain types of music being considered as torturous. Discussing the use of Britney Spears songs to dissuade pirates off the coast of Somalia, Steven Jones of the Security Association for the Maritime Industry said: 'I'd imagine using Justin Bieber would be against the Geneva Convention' (Radnedge, 2013). This statement considers Bieber's music as lacking in substance, perhaps 'naff', and appealing to a shared understanding of this opinion, so that what is a potential violation of human rights conventions becomes humorous. A person's hearing can become damaged when the frequency of a sound exceeds 20,000 hertz, whether that be heavy metal, cheesy pop music or a children's TV theme tune; any music or sound over a certain volume can cause harm. As Attali (1984, p. 27) argues 'in biological reality, noise is a source of pain. Beyond a certain limit, it becomes an immaterial weapon of death'.

There has been history of using music particularly, but also sound, for reprehensible reasons[7]. One example was the use of music during Nazi Germany in concentration and death camps (Moreno, 2006) and the ghettos of various Eastern Europe cities (Gilbert, 2005). Despite sometime music being used for positive reasons among the prisoners (Flam, 1992), often it was used to accompany death and torture (Brauer, 2016). The use of music during the Vietnam War is well known, possibly due to the cultural significance of it in American films such as *Apocalypse Now* (1979) which uses Wagner's *Ride of the Valkyries* to accompany the airborne destruction of a North Vietnamese village (Wilson, 2018) an act illustrative of the real use of music during that conflict (Andresen, 2003).

Technological advances have meant that amplified music and sound have been used in inventive ways in consequential conflicts, for example, very loud music was played to intimidate and torture during conflicts such as US interventions in Guatemala[8] and Panama[9] and during the invasions of Afghanistan in 2001 and in Iraq in 2003, US troops constructed sound systems in their military vehicles with speakers hooked up to their CD players (Pieslak, 2007; Cusick, 2006). Reports from Myanmar suggest there has been widespread torture of dissenters following a military coup in February 2021 (Harding, 2021) while in China, Uighur detainees in camps have been tortured horrifically, and while this might be less harmful than other treatment they have received, there are reports of the forced singing of patriotic Chinese songs (Hill et al., 2021), illustrating that music as torture is still currently exploited by repressive states.

Although music is still being used in this manner, it appears to attract less public attention than previously, but it seems that in many places, where there is conflict, the powerful will find ways to harm and denigrate. The use of music as torture is an obvious human rights violation; under Article 3 'everyone has the right to life, liberty and security of person', while Article 5 states that 'no one shall be subjected to torture or to cruel, inhuman or degrading treatment or punishment'. Modern human rights drawn from the theoretical roots of liberal democracy[10] were formalised by the United Nations General Assembly in 1948. The Universal Declaration of Human Rights (UDHR), conceived as a statement of objectives to be followed by governments was signed by 38 countries. Closely following this development was the Geneva Convention in 1949 which laid down requirements for the treatment of prisoners of war. There are geographically specific human rights conventions, for example American, African and European Conventions on human rights designed to address different cultural dimensions (Hansungle, 2010). There are also a number of additional agreements regarding specific issues such as the United Nations Convention against Torture (UNCAT) and the United Nations Convention on the Rights of the Child (UNCRC). Two other important treaties, the International Covenant on Civil and Political Rights (ICCPR) which commits states to recognise civil and political freedoms, such as the right to vote, and the International Covenant on Economic, Social and Cultural Rights (ICESCR) which focuses on freedom of speech, and social, economic, and cultural rights, such as food, education, health, and the right to a cultural life, were introduced in 1976 (Macklem, 2015).

Intangible violence: Censorship

Criminologists are interested in how decisions are made about what activities and behaviours constitutes a human right, and also the differential implementation of rights once they are accepted as such. This is where the study of harms comes into play because even when specific laws are not being violated, the erosion of the protection of people's rights in terms of freedom and autonomy, which is one of the most common social injustices, can be instigated by the state. The United Nations has had a Special Rapporteur in the field of cultural rights since 2009, which highlights the importance of human rights in artistic expression and freedom, and the knowledge that music can reflect more important messages about problematic social arrangements and practices, rather than just being entertainment. The Universal Declaration of Human Rights (UNDHR) Article 27 states that 'everyone has the right freely to participate in the cultural life of the community, to enjoy the arts and to share in scientific advancement and its benefits'. Additionally, UNDHR Article 27 says that people have 'the right to the protection of the moral and material interests resulting from any scientific, literary or artistic production of which he is the author'. However, there are times when the law may interfere with this right.

When music has categorised as having negative consequences, then censorship can be a perceived answer. Laws regulate and discipline popular culture, but there are power issues inherent in whose, when, and what music is labelled as dangerous. This can then lead to an erosion of liberty, and a breach of an individual's right to freedom of expression. One example is the genre of heavy metal which has often been discussed relation to censorship; it has sometimes been subject to prohibition or suppression in many countries around the world, for example, Russia, China, and Malaysia (LeVine, 2010). However, it is not only less democratic countries where metal and other 'deviant' music is outlawed as the alleged links between listening to heavy metal and suicide or violence has a long history[11].

The way that music is suppressed is important criminologically because violations of the human rights of individuals and groups reveal serious social injustices. Artists can be censored, or side-lined, because of ideological or religious influences of the state, one example of this is Afghanistan. In 1996 the Taliban took control and issued rulings against music because of their conservative interpretation of Islam, which led to instruments and cassettes being destroyed (Baily, 2001). This followed a period of censorship in the late 1970s during Communist rule where music was severely censored. There were still restrictions into the post-Communist period (1992–1996) (Baily, 2001). Despite music schools and orchestras being re-established in the 2000s, the return to power of the Taliban in 2021 has meant a return to musicians' fearing for their lives and livelihoods (Wertheimer, 2021; Zitser, 2021).

The active censorship in countries such as China, Russia and North Korea are well documented (Human Rights Watch, 2021a, 2021b) where access to the internet and outside sources of information is closely managed by the state. The coronavirus pandemic appears to have been used by governments to curtail freedoms both physically and technologically, for example there were moves by some countries (Russia for example in addition to China which already does control internet content) to isolate the country from the international internet during national emergencies.

The growth of national sovereignty over controlling the internet is a fairly recent development. In 2013, the UN special rapporteur for promotion and protection of the right to freedom of opinion and expression aired concerns at the 'multiple measures taken by States to prevent or restrict the flow of information online' (La Rue, 2013, p. 3). According to Freedom House, a human rights advocacy organisation, global internet freedom has declined for the 10th consecutive year with the largest falloffs occurring in Myanmar and Kyrgyzstan (Shahbaz and Funk, 2020).

Music and musicians often find that they are prevented from performing if the authorities deem them too subversive. The first amendment of the US constitution guarantees freedoms concerning religion, expression and assembly, as do the constitutions of many other countries. There may be an implicit assumption towards free speech, via common-law (Davis, 2013; Gray, 2012) in others; for example, the UK was one such country until the Human Rights Act[12] actively protected the right to free speech (Lester, 2016). Despite these declared freedoms, there are inconsistencies between these and the lived experience of individuals and groups – countries do not have to be autocracies to censor music and musicians. Even where countries have enshrined free speech because it is a qualified right, it may be suspended to protect the rights of another or in the public interest. It can be considered reasonable to place restrictions on freedom of expression to prevent hate speech, although this is often contested as freedom of expression is a cornerstone right, in that it is one that enables other rights to be protected and exercised (Uran, 2010).

One way for states to bypass freedom of speech rights arguments is to invoke legitimate control of deviancy. Defining music as dangerous or offensive is an exercise in power which allows for its limitation and surveillance and what occurs is a form of control over the population's cultural access (Korpe et al., 2006). Although the US has the first amendment under which most artistic expression is protected, material considered obscene is not protected. *Miller v California, 413 U.S. 15 [1973]* defines obscene as that which is 'without socially redeeming value' and lacking 'serious literary, artistic, political, or scientific value' (known as the SLAPS test) (Nuzum, 2005). Material deemed 'harmful to minors' is also not covered by the first amendment and music lyrics can be designated as 'inciteful speech' (Fischer, 2003) and again outside the remit of free speech.

There have been laws against obscenity in the UK since the late 1700s. In 1959 the Obscene Publications Act was passed in England and Wales which defined obscenity somewhat vaguely as 'content whose effect will tend to deprave and corrupt those likely to read, see or hear it' (Corrin and Gask, 2009, p. 147). The European Court of Human Rights has recognised that convictions under the Obscene Publications Act 1959 interferes with individuals' Article 10 rights to free expression. However, because the European Convention right can be restricted to protect 'morals in a democratic society' this can allow for obscenity prosecutions under the OPA, which still occur regardless of artistic or literary merit. Additionally, financial demands for the policing of controversial plays, concerts or exhibitions may be increased, jeopardising the economic feasibility of the event (Index on Censorship, 2020). Police may also 'advise' against a show owing to security concerns and often incentivises venues to reconsider hosting the event (Jonze, 2010). For example, concerts by artists from certain musical genres may be banned because authorities cite potential unrest and disorder should they occur (Horsfall, 2013; Topping, 2012; Gray, 2010). The Metropolitan Police used form 696, a risk assessment form when considering event licenses[13], to gage whether there was potential harm arising from the music concert and the potential for public order issues. However, the form mainly seemed to curtail grime and drill concerts music (Fatsis, 2019) and there were accusations of racial profiling because the form explicitly asked what music style will be played at proposed events and were particularly focused on event predominantly featuring DJs or MCs, therefore targeting genres such as grime, bashment, and garage (Olutayo, 2017).

If artists find it problematic to perform, then they can release their own music and videos. This can be done without the support of the formal music industry as artists can record, edit, and distribute using social media and the internet. A common way to distribute is through sharing on YouTube. However, there are restrictions to what social media platforms will host. For example, YouTube's Community Guidelines state 'hate speech, predatory behaviour, graphic violence, malicious attacks and content that promotes harmful or dangerous behaviour isn't allowed on YouTube' (YouTube's Community Guidelines, 2021). Although the guidelines state that receiving a report does not mean content is automatically taken down, the service is susceptible to pressure from police and other guardians if they deem content violent, something a number of drill artists have experienced (Waterson, 2018).

There is a disparity on the genres of music that are removed from social media platforms for violence. Discussing murder ballads[14], Newman (2020) argues that these songs are ways that performers and listeners can 'play out socially inappropriate taboos ... taking on themes such as murder in a safe and controlled manner ... without judgment or threat of punishment' (Newman, 2020, p. 10). However, while it is OK for Nick Cave to do this, Digga D cannot (Clowes, 2021; Newman, 2017). Thapar (2019) argues that this is an authoritarian clampdown, because there is only a hazy relationship between drill and actual violence. There has been a long history of the suppression of black musical genres, documented particularly in the US which saw black culture from jazz to rap construed as morally problematic (Johnson, 1994; Rose, 1985) but there is also to a growing analysis in the UK about the silencing of black culture (Fatsis, 2019; Bernard, 2018). Not dissimilar to the vilification of rap, particularly in the 1980s and 1990s (Rose, 1994), grime and drill in UK have come under scrutiny. Cressida Dick, the then-commissioner of the Metropolitan Police has singled out drill music as having 'a terrible effect' on gang violence' (Wright and Mills, 2018) and the police have argued that removal of videos is a proportionate, legitimate limitation to the right to freedom of expression.

However, decoding music is problematic, as often the judgement of 'danger' focuses on words, and is predisposed to interpretation, such as perceptions of misogynistic lyrics in rap, gang 'beef' in drill and songs about satanism and violence in death metal (Brabazon, 2012; Gray, 2010; Weinstein, 2000; Tatum, 1999). Freedom of expression is an important aspect of human rights, and artistic expression is protected because of its recognised importance for individual fulfilment and as a means of communicating and developing ideas. Critics of censorship, such as the organisation Liberty, highlight the 'chilling effect' that disproportionate restriction can have on expression (Tambini et al., 2008).

Conclusion

This chapter has considered how the state and corporations use, abuse, and control music and those who make it, play it, and listen to it. The consideration of this issue from a criminological perspective is useful in terms of analyses of power, rights, and harm. The misuse of music for torture and harm is a blatant contravention of human rights articles and conventions. Music has been part of 'enhanced interrogation' torture techniques which are designed to leave little, if any physical trace. Psychological torture is frequently problematic to establish despite often being more damaging in the longer term than physical torture (Reyes, 2007). The use of music as a weapon in war and conflict or as punishment takes something society generally perceives as intrinsically 'good' (Lesiuk, 2010) and subverts it for reprehensible purposes.

Power is wielded when certain sounds or 'noise' can be heard, while the noise others can make is reduced by means of surveillance and social control (Attali, 1984). Presdee (2000, p. 17) says that the powerful define 'what music is carnival and what is not; where and when it is played and where not'; distinctions which often result in restrictions to speech and expression. States, their agents and corporations have the power to control and to define some music as deviant or offensive and therefore restrict it, suppress it, or subject it to an outright ban, and different genres of music experience this censure inequitably.

Freedom of speech and expression are important issues because they reinforce all other human rights and are essential for society to be able to discuss, debate, and effect change. The curtailment of expression and cultural innovation is a problematic one in free democratic countries as well as in obviously more repressive states, as is the use of violence by states and their agents (LeVine, 2017). Political censorship can be understood predominantly in terms of censorship, occurring through laws, and interpretations of those laws; however, moral censorship of musicians is also exercised through social movements and economic pressures.

Notes

1 First-generation rights are concerned with individual's property and curbing the excesses of the state. Second-generation identified bas social and cultural rights, but while governments may have a duty to support these, they remain resource dependent.

2 The social harms perspective is a fundamental part of critical criminology. Zemiology (from the Greek for harm) is a growing perspective within criminology, although some consider it should be considered a separate discipline (Hillyard and Tombs, 2017).

3 Powerful agents may be state agents, but can often be outside of this, such as powerful corporations, etc.

4 Three young men, Ruhal Ahmed, Shafiq Rasul and Asif Iqbal from Tipton in the English West Midlands were captured in Afghanistan as 'enemy combatants' in 2001 and transported to Guantanamo Bay. They were released without charge and returned to the UK in 2004.

5 A stress position places the human body so that a great amount of weight is placed on just one or two muscles.
6 There is some opposition to the use of their music for the purposes of torture by bands such as Rage Against the Machine and others who formed a pressure group Zero dB to challenge this (Swash, 2008).
7 Music has been used in war for a long time (Meilinger, 2016).
8 CIA techniques consisted of physical and sensory assaults, with extreme temperature changes, strobe lighting and loud, irregular sounds and music blasted at the prisoner (Ortiz and Harbury, 2006).
9 The US army played loud heavy metal to remove Noriega from his hiding place during the December 1989 invasion to depose him (Goodman, 2010).
10 The work of social contract theorists such as Hobbes and Locke, but a focus on individual freedoms and state sovereignty poses some problems for the extension of rights across all countries and cultures (Goodale, 2018).
11 Ozzy Osborne was sued in a US court over his song *Suicide Solution*, and Judas Priest was accused of suicide-inducing hidden messages on an album (Wright, 2000).
12 The Human Rights Act 1998 enshrines the European Convention of Human Rights into UK legislation.
13 Metropolitan Police's Promotion and Event Assessment Form, commonly known as Form 696, was in operation for over 10 years in London (Barnard, 2019).
14 Murder ballads have roots in the folk ballads of Britain but is particularly well known in the US when settlers merged this with the music of African Americans in some southwestern US states (Hastie, 2011; Perryman, 2013).

References

Amnesty International (2021) USA: Right the wrong: Decision time on Guantanamo. https://www.amnesty.org/en/documents/amr51/3474/2021/en/#:~:text=This%20 report%20returns%20to%20the,the%20lifetime%20of%20this%20prison [Accessed 25/09/21].

Andresen, L. (2003) *Battle Notes: Music in the Vietnam war*. Brule, WI.: Savage Press.

Apocalypse Now (1979, film) Directed by Francis Ford Coppolla. Los Angeles, USA: United Artists.

Attali, J. (1984) *Noise: The political economy of music*. Manchester: University of Manchester Press.

Baily, J. (2001) *"Can you stop the birds singing?" The censorship of music in Afghanistan*. Copenhagen: Freemuse.

BBC (2013) BBC defends Baroness Thatcher Ding Dong song decision. *BBC News*, 12 April. http://www.bbc.co.uk/news/uk-22126940 [Accessed 21/05/2016].

Bernard, J. (2018) Form 696 is gone – So why is clubland still hostile to black Londoners? *The Guardian*, 31 January. https://www.theguardian.com/music/2018/ jan/31/form-696-is-gone-so-why-is-clubland-still-hostile-to-black-londoners [Last Accessed 22 March 2021].

Biancorosso, G. (2004) Film, music, and the redemption of the mundane. In Washburne, C.J. and Derno, M. (Eds.) *Bad music: The music we love to hate* (pp. 190–211). London: Routledge.

Borger, J. (2003) Metallica is latest interrogation tactic. *The Guardian*, 20 May. https://www.theguardian.com/world/2003/may/20/iraq.julianborger [Last Accessed 30 December 2020].

Bourdieu, P. (2010 [1995]) *Distinction: A social critique of the judgement of taste.* London: Routledge.

Brabazon, T. (2012) *Popular music: Topics, trends and trajectories.* London: Sage.

Brauer, J. (2016) How can music be torturous? Music in Nazi concentration and extermination camps. *Music and Politics*, X (1). DOI: 10.3998/mp.9460447.0010.103

Clowes, E. (2021) For British drill stars, the police are listening closely. *New York Times*, 11 January. https://www.nytimes.com/2021/01/11/arts/music/digga-d-drill-music.htm [Last Accessed 21 January 2022].

Cohen, S. (1985) *Visions of social control: Crime, punishment and classification.* Cambridge: Polity.

Cohen, S. (1993) Human rights and crimes of the state: The culture of denial. *Australia and New Zealand Journal of Criminology*, 26, pp. 97–115.

Corrin, L. and Gask, A. (2009) Powers to stop, search, enter and seize. In Colvin, M. and Cooper, J. (Eds.) *Human rights in the investigation and prosecution of crime* (pp. 113–156). Oxford: Oxford University Press.

Cusick, S.G. (2006) Music as torture/music as weapon. *Transcultural Music Review*, 10 https://irenetaylortrust.files.wordpress.com/2019/03/sounding-out-evaluation-2016-2018.pdf. [Last Accessed 10 May 2019].

Davis, H. (2013) *Human rights law.* Oxford. Oxford University Press.

DeNora, T. (2004) *Music in everyday life.* Cambridge: Cambridge University Press.

DeNora, T. (2010) *After Adorno: Rethinking music sociology.* Cambridge: Cambridge University Press.

Fatsis, L. (2019) Policing the beats: The criminalisation of UK drill and grime music by the London Metropolitan Police. *The Sociological Review*, 67 (6), pp. 1300–1316.

Fischer, P.D. (2003) *What if they gave a culture war and nobody came? Prospects for free musical expression in the United States.* Freemuse. https://freemuse.org/graphics/Publications/PDF/fischer28012003.pdf [Accessed 11/08/2017].

Flam, G. (1992) *Singing for survival: Songs of the Lodz ghetto, 1940–45.* Champaign: University of Illinois Press.

Freeman, M. (2017) *Human rights*, 3rd ed. Cambridge: Polity.

Gilbert, S. (2005) *Music in the holocaust: Confronting life in the Nazi ghettos and camps.* Oxford: Clarendon Press.

Gilman, L. (2010) An American soldier's iPod: Layers of identity and situated listening in Iraq. *Music and Politics*, 4 (2), pp. 1–17.

Goodale, M. (2018) The myth of universality: The UNESCO "Philosophers' Committee" and the making of human rights. *Law and Social Inquiry*, 43 (3), pp. 596–617.

Goodman, S. (2010) *Sonic warfare. Sound, effect and the ecology of fear.* Cambridge, MA: MIT Press.

Gray, A. (2012) Racial vilification and freedom of speech in Australia and elsewhere. *Common Law World Review*, 41 (2), pp. 167–195. DOI: 10.1350/clwr.2012.41.2.0236

Gray, L. (2010) Can music kill? *Index on Censorship*, 39 (3), pp. 112–120.

Green, P.J. and Ward, T. (2000) State crime, human rights, and the limits of criminology. *Social Justice*, 27 (1), pp. 101–115.

Hansungle, M. (2010) The historical development of international human rights. In Chowdhury, A.R. and Bhuiyan, J.H. (Eds.) *An Introduction to International Human Rights Law* 1 (pp. 3–6). Leiden: Brill.

Harding, L. (2021) Outrage in Myanmar after activist allegedly tortured to death Outrage in Myanmar after activist allegedly tortured to death. *The Guardian*, 15 March. https://www.theguardian.com/world/2021/mar/15/the-death-of-zaw-myat-lynn-allegations-torture-used-on-opposition-activist-in-myanmar [Accessed 19/03/2021].

Hastie, C.R. (2011) *This murder done: Misogyny, femicide, and modernity in 19th-century Appalachian murder ballads.* Master's Thesis, University of Tennessee. https://trace.tennessee.edu/utk_gradthes/1045 [Accessed 30/11/21].

Hill, M., Campanale, D. and Gunter, J. (2021) 'Their goal is to destroy everyone': Uighur camp detainees allege systematic rape. *BBC News*. https://www.bbc.co.uk/news/world-asia-china-55794071 [Accessed 19/03/2021].

Hillyard, P. and Tombs, S. (2017). Social harm and zemiology. In Leibling, A. Maruna, S. and McAra, L. (Eds.) *The Oxford Handbook of Criminology* (pp. 284–305). Oxford: Oxford University Press.

Hirsch, L. (2007) Weaponizing classical music: Crime prevention and symbolic power in the age of repetition. *Journal of Popular Music Studies*, 9 (4), pp. 342–358.

Hirsch, L. (2011) "Do you really want to hurt me?" Music as punishment in the United States legal system. *Popular Music and Society*, 34 (1), pp. 35–53.

Hirsch, L. (2012) *Music in American crime prevention and punishment.* Ann Arbor: University of Michigan Press.

Hodgkinson, P. (2002) *Goth: Identity, style and subculture.* Oxford: Berg.

Horsfall, S.T. (2013) Understanding deviant music. In Deflem, M. (Ed.) *Music and Law.* Bingley: Emerald Books.

Human Rights Watch (2021a) China World Report. https://www.hrw.org/world-report/2021/country-chapters/china-and-tibet [Accessed 14/09/2021].

Human Rights Watch (2021b) Russia World Report. https://www.hrw.org/world-report/2021/country-chapters/russia [Accessed 14/09/2021].

Idrobo-Ávila, E.H., Loaiza-Correa, H., van Noorden, L., Muñoz-Bolaños, F.G. and Vargas-Cañas, R. (2018) Different types of sounds and their relationship with the electrocardiographic signals and the cardiovascular system. *Frontiers in Physiology*, 9, p. 525. DOI: 10.3389/fphys.2018.00525

Index on Censorship (2020) *Free speech & the law: Obscene Publications.* https://www.indexoncensorship.org/2020/01/free-speech-and-the-law-obscene-publications/ [Accessed 25/04/2021].

Johnson, L. (1994) Silencing gangsta rap: Class and race agendas in the campaign against hardcore rap lyrics. *Temple Political and Civil Rights Law Review*, 3, p. 25.

Jonze, T. (2010) Rapper Giggs's tour cancelled after police warning. *The Guardian*, 23 February. https://www.theguardian.com/music/2010/feb/23/rapper-giggs-tour-cancelled [Accessed 19/03/2021].

Keating, J. (2008) U.S. metal band happy to help torture prisoners. *Foreign Policy Magazine*. https://foreignpolicy.com/2008/12/11/u-s-metal-band-happy-to-help-torture-prisoners/ [Accessed 06/09/2021].

Korpe, M., Reitov, O. and Cloonan, M. (2006) Music censorship from Plato to the Taliban. In Brown, S. and Volgsten, U. (Eds.) *Music and manipulation: On the social uses and social control of music* (pp. 239–263). New York: Bergham Books.

Kotarba, J.A. (2009) 'I'm just as Rock 'n' Roll fan.' Popular music as a meaning resource for aging. *Civitas - Revista de Ciências Sociais*, 9 (1), pp. 118–132.

La Rue, F. (2013) *Report of the Special Rapporteur on the promotion and protection of the right to freedom of opinion and expression*. Human Rights Council twenty-third session. A/HRC/23/40.

Lesiuk, T. (2010) The effect of preferred music on mood and performance in a high-cognitive demand occupation. *Journal of Music Therapy*. 47 (2), pp. 137–154. DOI: 10.1093/jmt/47.2.137

Lester, A. (2016) *Five ideas to fight for: How our freedom is under threat and why it matters*. London: Oneworld Publications.

LeVine, M. (2010) Headbanging against repressive regimes: Censorship of heavy metal in the Middle East, North Africa, Southeast Asia and China (Freemuse, report no. 9). Copenhagen, Freemuse.

LeVine, M. (2017) Enraged and defiant: Revolutionary artists against the state in Morocco and Egypt. In Kirkegaard, A. et al. (Eds.) *Researching Music Censorship* (pp. 52–82). Cambridge: Cambridge Scholars Press.

Macklem, P. (2015) *The sovereignty of human rights*. Oxford University Press.

Meilinger, P.S. (2016) Sound and war. *The RUSI Journal*. 161 (5), pp. 78–83.

Moreno, J.J. (2006) Orpheus in hell: Music in the holocaust. In Brown, S. and Volgsten, U. (Eds.) *Music and manipulation: On the social uses and social control of music* (pp. 264–286). Oxford: Bergham Books.

Newman, D. (2017) Murder ballads: Nick Cave and his approach to killing in song. *Musicology Australia*, 39 (2), pp. 96–115. DOI: 10.1080/08145857.2017.1393149

Newman, D. (2020) Murder ballads and death in song. *Australian Feminist Law Journal*, 46 (1), pp. 17–38. DOI: 10.1080/13200968.2019.1810894

New York Times (1992) Germany acts to ban songs by 5 neo-Nazi rock groups. *New York Times*, 3 December. http://www.nytimes.com/1992/12/03/world/germany-acts-to-ban-songs-by-5-neo-nazi-rock-groups.html [Accessed 10/08/2017].

New York Times Opinion (1994) Music of hate. *New York Times*, 8 February. http://www.nytimes.com/1994/02/08/opinion/music-of-hate.html [Accessed 06/08/2017].

Nuzum, E. (2005) *Singing in the echo chamber: Music censorship in the U.S. after September 11th*. Copenhagen: Freemuse.

Olutayo, V. (2017, April 6) Form 696 and why grime is not the enemy. *Independent*. http://www.independent.co.uk/arts-entertainment/music/features/form-696-police-uk-music-venues-grime-music-discrimination-comment-a7670436.html [Accessed 16/10/2017].

Ortiz, D. and Harbury, J. (2006) *Torture by the United States of America: The Survivors' Viewpoint*. Submitted to the United Nations Human Rights Committee in Response to the 28 November 2005 Report of the United States of America by the Torture Abolition and Survivor Support Coalition International. https://www.google.com/url?sa=i&rct=j&q=&esrc=s&source=web&cd=&cad=rja&uact=8&ved=0CAQQw7AJahcKEwjwnZPVhtH7AhUAAAAAHQAAAAAQAw&url=https%3A%2F%2Fwww2.ohchr.org%2Fenglish%2Fbodies%2Fhrc%2Fdocs%2Fngos%2Ffinal_iccpr_tasscreport.doc&psig=AOvVaw3ZvR1A18Fh7aeFCEyD7Rx0&ust=1669730952105555 [Last accessed 30 March 2022].

Perryman, C W. (2013) *Africa, Appalachia, and acculturation: The history of bluegrass music*. Graduate Theses, Dissertations 298. https://core.ac.uk/outputs/230453310 [Accessed 21/05/2021].

Pieslak, J.R. (2007) Sound targets: Music and the war in Iraq. *Journal of Musicological Research*, 26 (2–3), pp. 123–149.

Piesner, D. (2006) Music as torture: War is loud. *Spin Magazine*, 30 November. https://www.spin.com/2006/11/music-torture-war-loud/ [Last accessed 26 April 2018].

Presdee, M. (2000) *Cultural Criminology and the carnival of crime*. London: Routledge.

Radnedge, A. (2013) Britney Spears songs used to scare off pirates in Somalia. *Metro. co.uk*, 27 October. http://metro.co.uk/2013/10/27/britney-spears-songs-used-to-scare-off-pirates-in-somalia-4163217/ [Accessed 25/11/2016].

Reyes, H. (2007) The worst scars are in the mind: Psychological torture. *International Review of the Red Cross*, 89 (867), pp. 591–617.

Rose, R. (1985) Eight elements of Jazz in improvisation. *Music Educators Journal*, 71 (9), pp. 46–47.

Rose, T. (1994) *Black noise: Rap music and black culture in contemporary America*. Middletown, CT: Wesleyan University Press.

Salmi, J. (2004) Violence in democratic societies: Towards an analytic framework. In Hillyard, P., Pantazis, C., Tombs, S. and Gordon, D. (Eds.) *Beyond Criminology: Taking Harm Seriously*. London: Pluto.

Shahbaz, A. and Funk A. (2020) *Freedom on the Net 2020: The pandemic's digital shadow*. https://freedomhouse.org/report/freedom-net/2020/pandemics-digital-shadow [Accessed 27/02/2021].

Smeulers, A.L. and Niekerk, S. (2009) Abu Ghraib and the war against terror – A case against Donald Rumsfeld. *Crime, Law and Social Change*, 51, pp. 327–349. DOI: 10.1007/s10611-008-9160-2

Smyczek, P.J. (2005) Regulating the battlefield of the future: The legal limitations on the conduct of psychological operations under public international law. *Air Force Law Review*, 57, pp. 209–240.

Songs of War (2012) A&O Buero film produktion for Al Jazeera.

Stafford Smith, C. (2008) Welcome to 'the disco'. *The Guardian*, 19 June. https://www.theguardian.com/world/2008/jun/19/usa.guantanamo [Accessed 17/10/2020].

Swash, R. (2008) Musicians tell US to ban using songs as torture. *The Guardian*, 10 December. https://www.theguardian.com/music/2008/dec/10/stop-the-music-torture-initiative [Accessed 06/08/2017].

Tambini, D., Leonardi D. and Marsden, C. (2008) *Codifying cyberspace: Communications self-regulation in the age of internet convergence*. London: Routledge/ Glasshouse.

Tasioulas, J. (2013) Human Rights, legitimacy, and international law. *The American Journal of Jurisprudence*, 58 (1), pp. 1–25. DOI: 10.1093/ajj/aut001

Tatum, B.L. (1999) The link between rap music and youth crime and violence: A review of the literature and issues for future research. *The Justice Professional* 11 (3), pp. 339–353.

Thapar, C. (2019) Don't censor drill music, listen to what it's trying to tell us. *The Guardian*, 6 February. https://www.theguardian.com/commentisfree/2019/feb/06/dont-censor-drill-music-listen-skengdo-am [Accessed 18/0/2021].

Thompson, M.S. (1997) *Beyond sound: Noise, affect and aesthertic moralism*. London: Bloomsbury.

Thompson, M.S. (2014) *Beyond unwanted sound: Noise, affect and aesthetic moralism*. PhD. thesis, University of Newcastle. https://theses.ncl.ac.uk/dspace/bitstream/10443/2440/1/Thompson,%20M.%2014.pdf [Accessed 15/08/2017].

Topping, A. (2012) Police accused of discriminating against urban music scene. *The Guardian*, 8 January. https://www.theguardian.com/music/2012/jan/08/police-accused-discriminating-urban-music [Accessed 12/08/2017].

Uran, P. (2010) Freedom of expression as the cornerstone of democracy. *International Journal of Arts and Sciences*, 3 (15), pp. 483–493.

Washburne, C. and Derno, M. (2004) *Bad music: the music we love to hate*. London: Routledge.

Waterson, J. (2018) YouTube deletes 30 music videos after Met link with gang violence. *The Guardian*, 29 May. https://www.theguardian.com/uk-news/2018/may/29/youtube-deletes-30-music-videos-after-met-link-with-gang-violence [Accessed 06/07/2018].

Weinstein, D. (2000) *Heavy metal: The music and its culture*. New York: Da Capo Press.

Wertheimer, T. (2021) Afghan music school falls silent under Taliban rule. *BBC*, 27 August. https://www.bbc.co.uk/news/world-asia-58344197 [Accessed 13/09/2021].

Wilson, A. (2018) How 'Apocalypse Now' etched Wagner's 'Ride of the Valkyries' into our brains forever. *Soundfly*, 1 February. https://flypaper.soundfly.com/discover/how-apocalypse-now-etched-wagners-ride-valkyries-into-our-brains/ [Last Accessed 4 July 2019].

Wright, R. (2000) I'd Sell You Suicide': Pop Music and Moral Panic in the Age of Marilyn Manson. *Popular Music*, 19 (3), pp. 365–385.

Wright, S. and Mills, E. (2018) YouTube removes 30 music videos after metropolitan police link them to gang violence. *The Telegraph*, 29 May. https://www.telegraph.co.uk/news/2018/05/29/youtube-removes-30-music-videos-metropolitan-police-links-gang/ [Accessed 16/08/2021].

YouTube (2021) Community Guidelines. https://www.youtube.com/intl/ALL_uk/howyoutubeworks/policies/community-guidelines/ [accessed 21/10/21]

Zitser, J. (2021) Taliban 'brutally' killed a popular Afghan folk singer just days after it said 'music is forbidden' in Islam, former minister says. *Insider*, 29 August. Afghanistan: Taliban kills popular folk singer days after music ban (businessinsider.com) [Accessed 13/09/2021].

8 Music in the Collective Lives of Prisoners

Chris Waller

Introduction

Music has had a long history in places of confinement and the prevailing image of a convict playing a harmonica or the sounds of Mozart's letter dance lilting through the exercise yard in the Shawshank Redemption (1994) have come to define the ways in which we think about this relationship. Music articulates a tension between liberty and constraint by drawing our attention towards forms of freedom that can exist in even the most restrictive circumstances. Yet while there is truth to this depiction of music as a resource for mitigating the 'pains of imprisonment' (Sykes, 1958), there is also a more complex and ambivalent history to music in carceral institutions. As accounts of slave ships (Skeehan, 2013; Thompson, 2014), plantations (Epstein, 1977), colonial regimes (Owlage, 2005) and penitentiaries (Waller, 2018) show, music has been frequently incorporated into the technologies of control and domination and brutal examples abound of enslaved people being forced to dance and sing for their captors. Amongst slave owners, the singing of enslaved people (often under duress) was used as a means of demonstrating their contentment as a count-argument to calls for abolition. In Europe, reformers such as John Hullah and Alexander Maconochie were convinced of music's capacity to instil moral dispositions in prisoners and colonial subjects and choirs, bands, and orchestras become commonplace across the expanding carceral state in the 19th century. As Owlage (2005) argues, the choir was first utilised amongst colonial subjects in South Africa as a disciplinary apparatus, allowing overseers to render subjects compliant by arranging them into functional parts of a greater whole. It is the view that music is able to access the most essential and spiritual aspects of the self (as well, paradoxically, as the most primitive parts) that has led it to become incorporated within these arrangements and these views still persist in some discourses to this day. Cusick's (2013) research on the more recent use of music to torture terrorist detainees illustrates the continuity of these techniques in contemporary carceral spaces and details how suspects are played loud, repeated songs for hours on end to induce extreme stress for the purpose of gathering intelligence.

DOI: 10.4324/9781003186410-8

While Cusick's account represents an extreme example, carceral spaces such as prisons use music as part of the disciplinary apparatus for ensuring compliance. Prisoners in England and Wales can access radios and stereos in addition to the National Prison Radio (NPR) station which can be accessed via in-cell television. In each of these cases, access is determined by a prisoner's conduct. Radios and stereos must be purchased from the prison canteen and, given the limited amount of weekly income they are able to receive, prisoners are often required to save for months at the expense of day-to-day comforts and necessities to afford these items. Music, therefore, represents a feature of the Incentives and Earned Privileges (IEP) system (maybe a footnote to explain a little more?) that incentivises prisoners to engage with the regime and maintain compliant behaviour.

While access has improved over the past decades with the inclusion of the NPR as a channel on in-cell televisions in England and Wales, the capacity for prisoners to use music as a reliable tool for stimulation and 'emotional regulation' (Gross, 2014; Laws and Crewe, 2016) is still very limited. Despite this, music constitutes an integral feature of the daily-life of prison in England and Wales and in carceral institutions across the world and the value of music as the basis for therapeutic and rehabilitative interventions is well established (Cox and Gelsthorpe, 2008; Caulfield, 2015; Cursley and Maruna, 2015; Urie et al., 2019; Crockett Thomas et al., 2021; Doxat-Pratt, 2021). In informal contexts too, music has been shown to provide a range of benefits for prisoners with studies suggesting that music is used to reconstruct and repair one's sense of self (Herrity, 2018; Hjørnevik and Waage, 2018) and can help to allay the various pains and stresses of imprisonment (Harbert, 2012; Herrity, 2014, 2018; Edri and Bensimon, 2019).

In the accounts outlined above, the focus tends to be on the role of music in individual life and across inter-personal relationships. Aside from Hjørnevik and Waage's (2018) study of music interventions in a low-security prison, collective practices that constitute part of the 'daily-life' of the prison are rarely subject to close examination. The aim of this paper is to contribute to these discussions by examining the role of music as part of the collective experience of imprisonment and draws on empirical research on the role of music in the daily life of a men's local prison. By examining the informal use of music, the paper seeks to explore how forms of affiliation, distinction, and connection occur within distinct social and material dynamics of the institution. While music can provide an important basis for shared experience and communality (Hesmondhalgh, 2013) the paper argues that we must remain guarded against simplistic understandings and remain attentive to the complex and ambivalent nature of music in spaces of confinement. The following section draws on existing research to provide a theoretical frame for examining the role of music within carceral spaces.

Music, sound, and identity

As many of the accounts outlined in the previous section suggest (Herrity, 2014, 2018; Hemsworth, 2016; Rice, 2016; Edri and Bensimon, 2019) due to the inherently leaky and resonant materiality of the prison, music is often experienced simultaneously as a desirable auditory stimulus and as a frustrating and persistent noise. Herrity (2018, p. 43) refers to music as both a 'means' and an 'obstacle' to negotiating prison life, drawing on accounts which describe the use of music to bully and distract prisoners. Hemsworth (2016) builds on Jewkes (2002) assertion that prisoners are held 'captive' by the material qualities of the prison, suggesting that prisoners have fewer resources for escaping their 'acoustic surroundings'. As Hemsworth suggests, the loud and complex sound of the prison'is amongst its most intimidating features for those who first enter and, for many, audio technologies are the only means to reduce the distressing noises heard when confined in one's cell. However, due to the proximity in which prisoners live as well as the acoustical properties of the prison environment, Hemsworth suggests that 'sonic solutions' for some can become 'sonic problems' for others as the acoustic space becomes 'overcrowded' (2016, p. 94)[2]. Rice (2016, p. 3) similarly notes how the access to amplified sound in the form of stereos and hi-fi's enables prisoners to 'intentionally or otherwise, to initiate sometimes lengthy and severe disturbances of one another's sonic space'. While outside the usual repertoire of political action, Rice suggests that this capacity to disturb the acoustic space of the prison illuminates areas in which institutional control is limited. As Herrity outlines in further detail, new options for knowledge and agency become available to prisoners who are able to 'attune' themselves to the acoustical characteristics of the prison space (Herrity in Herrity et al., 2021). While these authors provide useful and detailed exploration of sound and sensory emplacement within the prison more broadly, the distinct character of music, as opposed to sound or noise, as a feature of the prison environment is under explored. Music cannot be easily disentangled from the sensory dimensions of the prison and, as many of these studies suggest, there are numerous ways in which music and sound come to be experienced as effectively continuous with each other. However, as DeNora (2000) suggests, music has unique properties when compared other forms of 'cultural material' and can 'afford' or inhibit forms of agency which are distinct from other materials.

The most frequently discussed role of music in carceral spaces is as a tool for 'emotional regulation' (DeNora, 2000, 2013; Gross, 2014; Laws and Crewe, 2016). Edri and Bensimon (2019) discuss how music provides a 'mental escape route' from the pains of imprisonment, allowing prisoners to 'release' painful emotions and anxieties. Herrity (2014, 2018) and Rice (2016) have similarly referred to the capacity of music to help prisoners 'manage' and 'direct' their emotions, referring to the work of DeNora (2000) to conceptualise music as a 'technology of the self'. Here music acts as an 'accomplice' in 'attaining, enhancing, and maintaining desired states of feeling and bodily energy' as well as helping us move away from undesirable states (2000, p. 53). Music has properties such as rhythm, timbre, melody, words, tempo etc., which are used as 'referents' for emotional and physical states. The associations of up-tempo music with energetic feelings, for instance, allow subjects to identify a desired trajectory for their affective state and orient themselves in relation to the music. Drawing on interviews with music listeners, DeNora explains that her respondents:

> make [...] articulations between musical works, styles and materials on the one hand and modes of agency on the other, such that music is used, prospectively, to sketch aspired and partially imagined or felt states.
>
> (DeNora, 2000, p. 53)

The capacity to adjust one's physical and emotional state thus provide important resources for prisoners who find themselves forced into spatial, temporal, and affective regimes to which they are forced to adapt. While prisoners engage in constant forms of 'emotional regulation' (Gross, 2014; Laws and Crewe, 2016), for DeNora, it is the pronounced capacity for music to act as an 'aide memoire' (2000, p. 66) for ways of feeling that distinguishes it as the 'cultural material *par excellence* of emotion and the personal' (ibid, p. 46). The significance of these properties to the discussion of music in the collective life in the prison is in the ways in which they enable prisoners to present themselves both inwardly and to those around them. Herrity (2014, 2018), for instance, describes how prison deprives prisoners of a wide range of resources used for identity construction and impression management such as clothes, jobs, and relationships, creating challenges in both related to others and themselves. As previous accounts have shown, the social and institutional demands of imprisonment often force prisoners to adopt 'prison identities' (Schmid and Jones, 1991) as strategic adaptations to the contingent, risky, and unfamiliar environment. These identities may often be at odds with pre-prison identities, causing strain and distress for those forced to undertake constant work to maintain a particular 'front' (Schmid and Jones, 1991; Jewkes, 2005; De Viggiani, 2012; Laws and Crewe, 2016). As Herrity (2018) suggests, music 'carves out space' for prisoners to explore, maintain, and reassemble aspects of their identity, providing important resources for managing the complex and contradictory demands placed upon them. Music's capacity to enable communication and felt connections across both space and time is evident in her accounts of prisoners sharing music with their loved ones outside the prison walls. Here the capacity to share musical experience with those on the outside, as well as with one's former self, provided an important means of retaining connection to one's pre-prison self.

While Hjørnevik and Waage's (2018) study examined music as part of a therapeutic intervention in a low-security prison in Norway, their work provides useful insight into the intersection between music, space, and identity. Drawing on Crewe et al.'s (2014) concept of 'emotional zones' as well as the work of DeNora (2013), the authors describe how musical performance allowed subjects to perform different identities to each other. Through the gathering of performer and audience, male prisoners were able to experiment with more vulnerable representations of self, contesting the masculine norms which were enforced within other regions of the prison. The 'co-created' (Hjørnevik and Waage, 2018, p. 9) character of this identity work is significant for this examination of the collective life of the prison and similar practices are evident in Richard Bramwell's work. Bramwell's (2015) study of London's rap scene drew on the history of rap within aural cultures, emphasising the embeddedness of rap within social and cultural contexts. Working with prisoners as part of a rap workshop at HMP Coldingly, Bramwell (2018) explored the ways in which rap provided a space for Black prisoners to enunciate values and concerns relating to their lives in prison as well as finding ways to negotiate their religious identities alongside other aspects of themselves.

While these accounts provide useful theory for understanding how music corresponds to life inside of carceral spaces, there is little direct consideration of the ways in which music is felt and used in by prisoners on a collective level within the daily-life of the institution. While Hjørnevik and Waage (2018) and Bramwell (2018) provide some insight here, their studies were undertaken as part of formalised music activities and, as such, do not capture the every-day character of music as it occurs and is experienced by prisoners. Similarly, Herrity's (2014, 2018) account provides useful insight into the ways that music can structure collective identities and connection to communities outside the prison but does not provide detailed examination of how these identities occur within the prison's social context. The following sections seek to address this gap by drawing on empirical research gathered in a men's local prison in the south of England undertaken as part of a PhD thesis (Waller, 2020). The data for this project was gathered using quasi-ethnographic techniques over a period of nine-months and involved participant and non-participant observation as well as interviews with prisoners and staff. This project sought to provide insight into the phenomenology of music as part of the sensory and affective dynamics of the environment, as well as the sociological and psychological dynamics surrounding phenomena such as individual and group identities. The following section provides more detail on the research context before considering the ambivalent nature of collective affiliation within the prison.

Music and difference

In contrast to the classical studies of prison sociology in the middle half of the 20th century, the experience of contemporary imprisonment is more individualised with the forms of solidarity, exemplified in Sykes (1958) description of the 'inmate code', replaced by a more 'fragmented' (Crewe, 2009) and diverse prisoner population. The 'inmate code' describes a set of rules which governed relations between inmates and bound them together in opposition to the prison staff. As Crewe (2005, 2009) suggests, drugs have played an important role in breaking down this collective prisoner identity with the intensification of the illicit trade leading to the breakdown of trust amongst prisoners and new configurations of power and status within the prisoner society (cf. Gooch and Treadwell, 2020). In addition to the new configurations of power and status that have emerged due to the influx of increasingly addictive drugs, Liebling (2006) has noted the diminishing opportunities for collective political representation or action amongst prisoners with processes for formal complaints becoming increasingly bureaucratic. Similarly, the introduction of 'systems of self-governance' (Crewe, 2011) such as IEP and individualised sentence plans have added further to the fragmentation and individualisation of prison life by providing institutional arrangements for dealing with deprivations that were previously managed by prisoners collectively (Crewe, 2006).

These characteristics were evident in the prisoner society at HMP South Hill, a local prison providing for category B and C prisoners in the south of England, where the research for this study took place. Social life tended to be organised across region, ethnicity, religion, and age-cohort with the proximity of London creating a distinct regional culture within the prison. As a local prison, sentence length was also an important feature with people at either the beginning or the end of life-sentences often living alongside with those awaiting trial or sentencing as well as those on mid or short-term sentences. The prison functioned as a passing point for a majority of those residing in there and the unpredictability and transience of life within the prison was a primary characteristic referred to by respondents. Edward, for instance, who was nearing release, expressed concern about being housed next to a prisoner serving a 30-year life sentence describing the arrangement as 'dangerous', explaining: '[someone] could be jumping about going "ah I'm going home next week!" And [another person has] got 40 years left, he'd jump up and chop you to pieces'. Steve, who was just beginning a 15-year sentence, also found co-habiting with people who had drastically different sentence lengths problematic and referred to their different 'mindsets'. Steve noted the sense of 'liminality' (Jewkes and Laws, 2021) he experienced as a life-sentenced prisoner at South Hill, suggesting that others on his wing tended to have short-term mentalities: 'There's not a feel of anyone setting any roots down'. The lack of stability within the social and institutional structures of prison was also attributed to disparities in age and for prisoners in their 40s and 50s such as Steve the 'mindsets' of younger prisoners was often referred to with disdain. Ron, who was in his 50s, referred to some of the younger prisoners he encountered as 'rude' and described the strain of living with a cellmate in his early 20s.

> [My cellmate is] alright but he's young and hyped up and (sucks teeth). Sometimes it can be very hard but, I just go with it man. I'd like to have my own space but it's so hard.
>
> (Ron)

While age was clearly a source of division in cases such as these, unpacking prisoners' views on these issues often revealed age to be a proxy for a broader grouping of identities. Ollie described a 'massive difference' between those from urban and non-urbanised areas. While he refused to reduce these distinctions to skin colour, he referred also to racial differences between black and white prisoners as part of the same cultural division.

> they all hang around in gangs and they act like idiots … and I find that they have less manners, they don't really know how to talk to people, their communication skills are slightly lacking like.
>
> (Ollie)

Phillips' (2008, 2012) work provides a detailed account of intersectionality between racial, regional, and class-based identities in prison, and illustrates the ways in which urban culture is imported into the prison and adapted to meet its social and cultural challenges.

The representation of young people as 'hyped' or 'negative' (Jack, 50s) was thus bound up with more than age. These terms referred to a subculture of young, predominantly black and mixed-race men from urban areas who formed affiliations that tended to be based on geographic regions within the greater urban area. This 'on road' (Reid, 2022; Waller, forthcoming) culture represented a distinct formation within the prison and elicited negative views from those who were unaffiliated for a variety of reasons. As Zach, a young mixed-race prisoner from London suggested, these views were not always justified and the reference to 'gangs' in Ollie's account, for instance, was explained as 'the way they word things'.

> On my spur there might be a group of friends but because they're from [an urban] culture, they call themselves 'gang'. But they're not a gang, they've only just met each other.
>
> (Zach)

As Zach's account suggests perceptions applied from outside the group could be subject to distortion or misunderstanding and the association with these young men and a nihilistic 'gang culture' which threatened the prevailing conventions and hierarchies of respect took shape as much through interaction with music genres associated with these young men as with the young men themselves. Genres such UK Rap and Drill had attracted a large amount of media attention at the time through their association with youth violence and gang activity (cf. Fatsis, 2019; Ilan, 2020) and, while the young men evidenced diverse and considered tastes, non-affiliated prisoners would often draw on media representations of the music as violent and nihilistic to portray these groups.

You hear what these boys, especially the young black lads, are listening to … it's no wonder they're running around stabbing each other – it makes *me* wanna kill people, you know?!

(Jack)

Everything they rap about is 'ah,' you know, tying this person up, and stabbing this person, you know? There's no positive in it really. It's all quite negative, you know? They don't think nothing about running in your house and tying your parents up and stabbing people, or taking another bloke's girlfriend off them. You know? Stuff that I was taught is just completely wrong.

(Ollie)

[A]ll the rapping and grime and that, I can never relate to that sort of stuff because I ain't from London. I'm from Hampshire. So, erm, like up here it's all like people get stabbed and all this and I don't deal with any of that. It's all this gang culture and that, I don't deal with any of it.

(Liam)

As the accounts above suggest, music constituted an important part of the cultural topography of the prison, providing ways for those on the periphery of these cultural formations to attempt to make sense of the urban youth cultures and masculine identities which they encountered. In this case, the properties of the music, both in terms of lyrical content and musical characteristics, served to articulate the perceived cultural distance between young urban dwellers, and older, predominantly white, men whose cultural sensibilities drew from different social and geographic domains. As we begin to see in these accounts, music was a cultural resource which enabled prisoners to navigate the transient and diverse social life of the prison. While, as the following section will show, music provided a means of identifying points of commonality between prisoners, it is important to illustrate here how music could also be used as a means of subjectification and social distinction (Bourdieu, 1979). Faced with the transient and insecure environment, music became a convenient signifier used in the practices of social and cultural ordering by some groups.

Collective life

While music operated as a cultural material of separation and distinction, it also provided a means of structuring feelings of togetherness and affiliation in various ways. Phillips (2012) has identified the significance of 'postcode identities' amongst some groups within the social life of the prison describing how these regional and class-based forms of 'solidarity' came to overlay other sources of identification such as race and ethnicity. Shared cultural and geographic experiences here provided a powerful basis of identification and these relationships were 'imported' (Irwin and Cressy, 1962; Phillips, 2012) into the social life of the prison creating the distinct groupings and lines of demarcation encountered in the previous section. For many of the young prisoners from London, for instance, the social life of the prison was continuous in many respects with that of their community and cliques tended to form on the basis of shared regional experiences and mutual acquaintances. The weekend rap shows on Capital FM and Radio One provided a significant landmark for younger prisoners who saw these shows as the focal point of their week. As Elias explained, 'You know how people on the outside, they'll go clubbing on the weekend, that's what they're looking forward to? Like, you see us, we're looking forward to [Charlie Sloth]' (Elias).

On spurs[3] with higher proportions of young prisoners the Charlie Sloth and Tim Westwood shows would be heard from every direction as young prisoners from London listened in to new releases and live performances by artists from their own areas. As Bramwell's (2015, p. 23) study of UK rap and grime culture has discussed, 'collective' practices of listening such as these enable young people to 'participate' in cultures from which they are geographically separated. The live character of these shows as well as the frequent shout-outs and references to familiar geographies and cultural experiences meant that young people were able to feel included in a wider cultural space and articulate aspects of their pre-prison identity (Schmid and Jones, 1991). Music reinforced the sense of cultural continuity with urban communities for young people, inflecting prison identities with regional characteristics and reinforcing the significance of urban geographies within the prison. While this could be the source of conflict in some instances with inter-regional rivalries imported into the prison (cf. Earle and Phillips,2015, it could also provide a basis for affiliation and the construction of stable relationships both inside and outside the prison (Jewkes, 2002; Herrity, 2014, 2018; Bramwell, 2018). For Tom, for instance, hearing the rest of the spur listening to the same radio shows as he did help him to identify himself as a 'normal guy' in relation to those around him. By hearing others express similar tastes, Tom was able to comfortably situate himself within the social and cultural life of his spur, normalising both himself and those around him despite their physical separation. For many, entering prison was experienced as a discontinuity from their previous lives and the social networks they inhabited, however, for many young men their social networks crossed over the prison walls providing both benefits and complications. Handling this continuity required a certain transparency and Elias described the need to 'prove yourself' and 'talk' to be verified within the prison's 'reputational network' (Crewe, 2009, p. 317). To be reticent or insincere about one's background or index offence would raise suspicion of holding rival allegiances or having been convicted for an offence deemed morally unconscionable (an example might be useful). As Elias explained, in addition to their value as spaces of communality and entertainment, the common gatherings on association to share rap verses were used as a means of scrutinising the integrity of those around them.

> You see rap, it's like ... you can relate to stuff innit? So you see (if) someone's rapping about something, like, they're rapping about something you get, and then [...] someone on the wing listens to you, they listen to us to see if you [are consistent].
>
> (Elias)

These collective practices involved a certain degree of policing which allowed groups of young people to ensure that those around them could be deemed trustworthy and appropriate for inclusion. The role of rap performances extended beyond this verificatory frame and there is more to be said about the broader cultural significance of these practices, both within and outside the prison (Bramwell, 2015, 2018), as well as the ways in which song-writing provided resources for adaptation (cf. Crockett Thomas et al., 2021). However, for now, this example further illustrates the fraught and transient world which prisoners inhabited and the distinctly defensive approaches towards interpersonal relations which permeated the seemingly most open and inclusive of practices. As Ricciardelli et al. (2015) suggest, unstable social environments lead prisoners into more defensive stances towards others making trusting relationships hard to form. For those relationships that do emerge, the high rates of churn at HMP South Hill meant that these were hard to maintain due to the constant pace of prisoner transferral and release.

Despite the pervasive distrust and transience which characterised the social life of the prison, there were occasional instances of relative stability in some regions of the prison. Steve, for instance, described how his neighbours on the third-floor of his cell maintained convivial relations with each other despite the diversity of cultures, ages, and sentence lengths. Steve described how he and his neighbours would sit out on the landings during association and listen to a radio brought out from a cell, describing this as a rare moment of relief from the stress of day-to-day life in prison.

> relaxing in prison is something you don't get to do very often. I'm not ... you are looking out for every ... everything's a little move. You might not get your right dinner at your fucking dinner time, you might not get your milk at lunch, you might not ... you've got to be on the ball constantly. So when you're up on that three's [third floor landing] and the doors open and you get that chance to relax with the people that you know, and you've got to know over the last few months, it's nice.
>
> (Steve)

Steve's account is redolent of Toch's (1977) concept of the 'niche' which describes the ways in which prisoners engage in the assembly of resources, spaces, and social relations into stabilised 'microcosms' used to render prison life more predictable. Music appeared to play a structuring role within this niche, providing a spatial and affective locus around which Steve and his friends would gather. Furthermore, the music provided a shared material for reminiscing and establishing points of shared experience, enabling the prisoners to build. For this reason, the music did not create an exclusive boundary around the group but rather allowed prisoners from other sections of the spur to approach and engage with them. Notably, Steve described how the young prisoners from urban areas would be amongst those walking up to the third-floor landing to comment on the music and join in with the reminiscing. As Steve suggested, the music would often remind the younger men of parents and family members, bridging sometimes the fraught relationships with the older prisoners and allowing them into the stable social arrangement of the niche.

> cos a couple of them come up, and then there might be a song that they recognise, and then like 'bloody hell, yeah!' Or it might be .... one feller used to come up and say 'ah, my nan used to have this on all the time', you know? Stuff like that. All music's got to strike a chord with someone somewhere, you know?
>
> (Steve)

The capacity for music to structure instances of collective engagement was seen in several further accounts, however, the stability and frequency of the collective practices described by Steve were not reported in similar terms elsewhere. To understand the collective life of the prison further we must look beyond these conventional understandings based around stable relationships, routine practices, and direct interaction towards the forms of connection that occur within a densely inhabited space with unique spatial and affective dimensions. By attuning ourselves towards the affective dimensions of the imprisonment the final section explores the ways in which forms of indirect connection between prisoners was afforded by music.

The affective dimensions of collective experience

Shaun explained that he would turn the volume of his in-cell television down to listen to the music played on his spur. Listening out for music offered a form of knowledge about the social and affective environment around him and he described one instance with an upstairs neighbour:

> I said to my cellmate the other day, I said 'he's playing some old-school house music, some real old classics', and he's only young. I bet you most of these songs was out before he was born, and I can hear him singing away so he's probably grown up with his parents listening to that song.
>
> (Shaun)

Despite having never spoken to this neighbour, hearing this familiar music allowed Shaun to theorise about the inhabitant of the upstairs cell and empathise with him despite their generational difference. For Shaun, hearing the frequent music and singing suggested that this younger prisoner was stressed with the general pressures of imprisonment and was using the music as an 'outlet' for his emotions. This practice of manipulating the volume of one's in-cell television and stereo was common amongst those interviewed in this study and reflects more than the desire to increase the variety of music available to them. As the example of the weekend radio shows suggests, collective listening practices were common despite the physical separation of cell walls. Even in moments of less affective intensity, music provided a constant backdrop for many of those who were interviewed allowing access to the affective dynamics of the collective life of the prison. While these instances were often fleeting and non-reciprocal, they constituted important moments of connection.

For those prisoners with radios, stereos, and hi-fis it was common to play their music for others on their spur or in the vicinity of their cell. While, in the case of Zach, this would be a matter of leaving his radio on so that his immediate neighbours could hear it while he was in education, for others such as Ollie there was a greater sense which music was being broadcast to a greater audience.

> The other night I had a cone, you know one of them cleaning cones, and I was playing Garage and House, and, like, in between I was MCing like a twat. And I was like, I was MCing as if I was in a nightclub, like, um, I'm not gonna give you an example because it's embarrassing ...
>
> (Ollie)

Ollie's performance often required him to perform the role of both MC and DJ and he described curating the music he played as if it were to a live audience. While it was common for music to be used as a way of blocking out noise from other parts of the prison, these instances illustrate another mode in which music was used as a means of extending the boundaries of the self beyond the enclosure of the cell. DeNora (2000, p. 102) has referred to the function of music here in terms of a 'prosthetic' and has described the capacity for music to provide a means for expressing forms of agency in a virtual space. Tobias differentiated between music played for personal consumption that 'pumped out' for collective consumption, suggesting that the broadcasted music tended to be selected on the basis of particular emotional and stylistic characteristics.

> If someone's pumping out a song in prison more than likely it's gonna be an upbeat song, or it's gonna be some sort of ... unless that person's going through particular woes this week (laughs) or something ... it's gonna be an upbeat song, otherwise he wouldn't really play it out loud like that.
>
> (Tobias)

Through the material manifestation of music as sound spreading across the prison, prisoners broadcasted their music as a way of putting themselves out into the world for whoever may wish to listen. While existing research (Herrity, 2018; Waller, 2020) has identified the use of music in the context of 'clashing' where prisoners, drawing on the idiom of soundsystem culture, attempt to out-do each other with the volume and quality of their music, these accounts articulate a different dimension to the use of music collective settings. Here the broadcasting of music seemed to serve both an individual and collective function, allowing broadcasters to expand the felt agency of the self while also contributing to the soundscape of the prison in a benevolent way. As both Tobias and Ollie suggested, the imagined audience constituted an important underpinning to these practices, allowing the broadcasters to inhabit particular roles and expressing their emotions or desired emotions to imagined others.

While many spoke of music as a source of pain, these accounts tend to refer to moments of discordance where activities or sleep were impeded upon by an overly loud or inappropriate sound rather than a continual frustration. Acknowledging these occasional tensions, Devonte suggested that 'on the whole', prisoners tended to 'appreciate' being able to hear music at any given point of the day. Will's description of music as something '*of* the prison' speaks further to the integral character of music to the experience of imprisonment, portraying it as a feature *of* imprisonment rather than something applied externally. Understanding the role of music alongside the collective lives of prisoners requires us to see music, in this way, as a deeply embedded feature of imprisonment that exists in continuity with the material, affective, social, and cultural 'flows' (Ingold, 2011) which constitute it.

Conclusion

To summarise, music holds an ambivalent and integral character within the collective lives of prisoners, providing important sources of shared experience but also marking distinctions and providing the means for exclusion and othering. Understanding the role of music here requires attention to the cultural contexts of prisons and their surrounding communities as music evidence an important bridge across the prison wall. We should therefore guard against common-sense understandings of music as a means of 'bringing people together' since the reality is far more complex.

Over the previous sections we have seen how music occurs as part of the cultural geography of the prison, providing both structure to existing relations of affiliation and distinction while also providing the means to transgress and reassemble these structures. While DeNora's (2000) characterisation of music as something that either 'affords' or 'inhibits' certain forms of cultural practice is accurate, it is important to note that within the collective lives of prisoners, music appears to be experienced both as a feature of the environment as well as a tool through which to navigate it. While music does enable forms of collective practice that occur in the face-to-face settings of the exercise yards and landings, given the large amount of time spent by prisoners in their cells it is important to consider forms of collective feeling, fleeting, and ambivalent though they may be, that occur between prisoners through the prison walls. The role of the sensory and spatial dimensions of imprisonment are important for understanding the ways in which music inhabits and structures the collectives lives of prisoners and emerging work in these areas provide complimentary theory for making sense of these phenomena. Crucially they draw our attention to the complex reality of music as a feature of the cultural, material, and social dynamics of the prison, opening up consideration of the ways in which music is felt and experienced by multiple subjects. Here, recent exploration of 'affective atmospheres' (Anderson, 2009; Riedel, 2015) may provide fruitful areas for future exploration of music in carceral spaces.

Notes

1 Due to the resonant qualities of much of the prison's designed features, metallic noises such as gates crashing open and shut, large metal doors, and keys jangling are commonly referred to as prominent features of the prison soundscape. (cf. Herrity, 2019, 2020).
2 The recent measure of providing prisoners with ear-plugs undertaken by HMP Buckley Hall led to a large reduction in violent incidents after prisoners were unlocked, further underscoring how significant music, and noise more broadly is to the well-being of prisoners (Inside Time, 2019).
3 A prison wing at HMP South Hill was divided into two or three 'spurs' containing three floors of cells with an open area in the middle and a small landing at the far end.

References

Anderson, B. (2009) Affective Atmospheres. *Emotion, Space and Society*, 2: 77–81.
Bourdieu, P. (1979) *Distinction: A Social Critique of the Judgement of Taste*. London: Routledge.
Bramwell, R. (2015) *UK Hip-Hop, Grime and the City*. The Aesthetics and Ethics of London's Rap Scenes. London: Routledge.
Bramwell, R. (2018) Freedom within Bars: Maximum Security Prisoners' Negotiations of Identity through Rap. *Identities*, 25(4): 475–492.
Cox, A. and Gelsthorpe, L. (2008) *Beats and Bars Music in prison: An evaluation*. Cambridge: Institutute of Criminology. http://www.artsevidence.org.uk/media/uploads/evaluation-downloads/mip-beats-&-bars-2008.pdf [Accessed 21 May 2022].
Crewe, B. (2006) The Orientations of Male Prisoners towards Female Officers in an English Prison. *Punishment and Society*, 8: 395–421.
Crewe, B. (2009) *The Prisoner Society. Clarendon Studies in Criminology*. Oxford: OUP.
Crewe, B (2011) Soft Power in Prison: Implications for Staff–Prisoner Relationships, Liberty and Legitimacy. *European Journal of Criminology*, 8(6): 455–468.

Crewe, B., Warr, J., Bennett, P., and Smith, A. (2014) The Emotional Geography of Prison life. *Theoretical Criminology*, *18*(1): 56–74.

Crockett Thomas, P., McNeill, F., Cathcart Fródén, L., Collinson Scott, J., Escobar, O. and Urie, A. (2021) Re-Writing Punishment? Songs and Narrative Problem-Solving. *Incarceration*.

Cusick, S. (2013) *Acoustemology of Detention in the 'Global War on Terror'*. In Georgina Born (Ed.) *Music, Sound and Space*, pp. 275–291. Cambridge: Cambridge University Press.

Cursley, J. and Maruna, S. (2015) A Narrative-Based Evaluation of "Changing Tunes" Music-based Prisoner Reintegration Interventions. *Changing Tunes*, http://www.artsevidence.org.uk/media/uploads/final-report-cursley-and-maruna-changing-tunes.pdf [Accessed 21/05/22].

DeNora, T. (2000) *Music in Everyday Life*. Cambridge: Cambridge University Press.

DeNora, T. (2013) *Music Asylums: Wellbeing through Music in Everyday Life.* Farnham: Ashgate.

De Viggiani, N. (2012) Trying to Be Something You Are Not: Masculine Performances within a Prison Setting. *Men and Masculinities*, *15*(3): 271–291.

Doxat-Pratt, S. (2021) Musical Communities in the Society of Captives: Exploring the Impact of Music Making on the Social World of Prison. *Musicae Scientiae*, *25*(3): 290–302.

Earle, R. and Phillips, C. (2015) Prison Ethnography at the Threshold of Race, Reflexivity and Difference. In Drake, D.H., Earle, R. and Sloan, J. (Eds.) *The Palgrave Handbook of Prison Ethnography*. Palgrave studies in prisons and penology, pp. 230–251. Basingstoke: Palgrave Macmillan.

Edri, O. and Bensimon, M. (2019). The Role of Music among Prisoners and Prison Staff: A Qualitative Research Study. *European Journal of Criminology*, *16*(6): 633–651.

Epstein, D. (1977) *Sinful Tunes and Spirituals: Black Folk Music to the Civil War.* London: University of Illinois Press.

Fatsis, L. (2019) Policing the Beats: The Criminalisation of UK Drill and Grime Music by the London Metropolitan Police. *The Sociological Review*, *67*(6): 1300–1316.

Gooch, K. and Treadwell, J. (2020). Prisoner Society in an Era of Psychoactive Substances, Organized Crime, New Drug Markets and Austerity. *The British Journal of Criminology*, 60: 1260–1281. DOI: 10.1093/bjc/azaa019.

Gross, J. (2014) *Handbook of Emotion Regulation*. New York: Guilford.

Harbert, B.J. (2012) *Follow Me Down: Portraits of Louisiana Prison Musicians (2012)*. Directed by Benjamin J. Harbert. New York: Films Media Group [DVD].

Hemsworth, K. (2016) 'Feeling the Range': Emotional Geographies of Sound in Prisons. *Emotion, Space, and Society*, *20*: 90–97.

Herrity, K. (2014) The Significance of Music to the Prison Experience. *Dissertation*. Royal Holloway, University of London.

Herrity, K. (2018) Music and Identity in Prison: Music as a Technology of the Self. *Prison Service Journal*, *239*: 40–47.

Herrity, K. (2020) Hearing Behind the Door: The Cell as a Portal to Prison Life. In Turner, J. and Knight, V. (Eds.) *The Prison Cell: Embodied and Everyday Spaces of Incarceration*, pp. 239–259. Cham: Palgrave Macmillan.

THerrity, K., Schmidt, B. and Warr, J. (2021) *Sensory Penalties*. Bingley: Emerald Publishing Limited.

Herrity, K.Z. (2019) Rhythms and Routines: Sounding Order in a Local Men's Prison through Aural Ethnography. Unpublished PhD Thesis. University of Leicester.

Hesmondhalgh, D. (2013) *Why Music Matters*. Chichester: Wiley Blackwell.

Hjørnevik, K. and Waage, L. (2019). The Prison as a Therapeutic Music Scene: Exploring Musical Identities in Music Therapy and Everyday Life in a Prison Setting. *Punishment and Society*, 21(4): 454–472.

Ilan, J. (2020) Digital Street Culture Decoded: Why Criminalizing Drill Music Is Street Illiterate and Counterproductive. *The British Journal of Criminology*, 60(4): 994–1013.

Ingold, T. (2011) *Being Alive: Essays on Movement, Knowledge, and Description*. Abingdon: Routledge.

Inside Time (2019) Ear Plugs Reduce Violence. *Inside Time*. Available at https:// insidetime.org/earplugs-reduce-violence/ [Accessed 18/03/2020].

Irwin, J. and Cressey, D. (1962) Thieves, Convicts and the Inmate Culture. *Social Problems*, 10(2): 142–155.

Jewkes, Y. (2002) *Captive Audience*. Abingdon: Routledge.

Jewkes, Y. (2005) Men Behind Bars: "Doing" Masculinity as an Adaptation to Imprisonment. *Men and Masculinities*, 8(1): 44–63.

Jewkes, Y. and Laws, B. (2021) Liminality Revisited: Mapping the Emotional Adaptations of Women in Carceral Space. *Punishment and Society*, 23(3): 394–412.

Rice, T. (2016) Sounds inside: prison, prisoners and acoustical agency. *Sound Studies*. 2: 1–15. 10.1080/20551940.2016.1214455.

Laws, B. and Crewe, B. (2016) Emotion Regulation among Male Prisoners. *Theoretical Criminology*, 20(4): 529–547.

Liebling, A. (2006). The Role of the Prison Environment in Prisoner Suicide and Prisoner Distress. In Dear, G.E. (Ed.) *Preventing Suicide and Other Harms in Prison*, pp. 103–117. London: Palgrave Macmillan.

Owlage, G. (2005) Discipline and Choralism: The Birth of Musical Colonialism. In Randall, A. (Ed.) *Music, Power, and Politics*: 25–46. Abingdon: Routledge.

Phillips, C. (2008) Negotiating Identities: Ethnicity and Social Relations in a Young Person's Institution. *Theoretical Criminology*, 12(3): 313–331.

Phillips, C. (2012) *The Multicultural Prison: Ethnicity, Masculinity, and Social Relations among Prisoners*. Oxford: Oxford University Press.

Ricciardelli, R., Maier, K. and Hannah-Moffat, K. (2015) Strategic Masculinities: Vulnerabilities, Risk and the Production of Prison Masculinities. *Theoretical Criminology*, 19(4): 491–513.

Reid, E. (2022) 'Trap Life': The Psychosocial Underpinnings of Street Crime in Inner-City London. *British Journal of Criminology*, DOI: 10.1093/bjc/azac004.

Riedel, F. (2015) Music as Atmosphere. Lines of Becoming in Congregational Worship. *Lebenswelt. Aesthetics and Philosophy of Experience*, 6: 80–111.

Schmid, T. and Jones, R. (1991) Suspended Identity: Identity Transformation in a Maximum Security Prison. *Symbolic Interaction*, 14(4): 415–432.

Shawshank Redemption (1994) Dir: Darabont, Frank. Columbia Film.

Skeehan, D. (2013) *Deadly Notes: The Atlantic Middle Passage and the Writing of the Middle Passage*, The Appendix. http://theappendix.net/issues/2013/7/deadly-notes-atlantic-soundscapes-and-the-writing-of-the-middle-passage [Accessed 19/12/2017].

Sykes G.M. (1958) *The Society of Captives: A Study of a Maximum Security Prison.* Princeton: Princeton University Press.

Thompson, K. (2014) *Ring Shout Wheel About: The Racial Politics of Music and Dance in North America Slavery.* Chicago: University of Illinois Press.

Toch, H. (1977) *Living in Prison: The Ecology of Survival.* New York: Macmillan.

Urie, A., McNeill, F., Frödén, L.C., Collinson-Scott, J., Thomas, P.C., Escobar, O. and McKerracher, G. (2019) Reintegration, Hospitality and Hostility: Song-Writing and Song-Sharing in Criminal Justice. *Journal of Extreme Anthropology, 3*(1): 77–101.

Waller, C. (2018) Darker than the Dungeon: Music Ambivalence and the Carceral Subject. *International Journal for Semiotics in Law, 31*: 275–299.

Waller, C. (2020) Tension and Release: Exploring the Role of Music in the Daily Life of a Men's Local Prison. PhD Thesis. Royal Holloway.

Waller, C. (Forthcoming) 'On Road Inside: Music and the Carceral Continuum' In Levell, J. and Earle, R. (Eds.) *On Road: Critical Questions of Youth Gender and Race.* Bristol: Bristol University Press.

9 The Benefits of Music Engagement Projects on Young People

A Music and Education Perspective

Justin Boreland and Eleanor Peters

Introduction: A brief history of the youth justice system in England and Wales

A distinct youth justice system emerged in the late Victorian period in England and Wales. Arguably, the first 'creation' of juvenile delinquency, at this point in history, children were perceived, contrariwise, both as a threat and as a victim, which is illustrated in welfare reform in the form of Factory Acts to protect child workers but also specific punitive laws for young people.[1] Elements of punishment and rehabilitation have co-existed from this time, for example, Reformatory Schools, established in 1854 aimed to redeem those who had already committed an offence; while Industrial Schools were targeted at a slightly younger group who were considered in danger of drifting into criminal activity.[2] In 1933 the Children and Young Persons Act replaces Reformatory Schools and Industrial Schools with government Approved Schools which were for those children and young people who had been convicted of criminal offences but also for those who were deemed to be beyond parental control (Bateman and Hazel, 2022). Both these, and the later Borstal regime had, at best mixed results (Cox, 2017; Field, 1969; Menis, 2012). The youth justice system has bounced between welfare and punitive approaches ever since[3] (Muncie, 2008) and fluctuations in the numbers of young people incarcerated often reflected this, for example, the welfare approach of 1960s resulted in fewer imprisonment of young people while the 'short sharp shock' approach in the 1970s and early 1980s led to rise in detainee numbers (Shaw, 1985) and an emphasis on 'just deserts' and individual responsibility informed approaches throughout the 1980s and early 1990s.

The new labour years and beyond

The increase in managerialism and target setting which began in the early 1990s under the Conservative government (Nash and Savage, 1995) continued apace following the 1997 election victory of Tony Blair's New Labour party. What followed was a complete overhaul of the youth justice system

DOI: 10.4324/9781003186410-9

and the passing of a plethora of new laws, elements of which singularly targeted young people, most notably the 1998 Crime and Disorder Act.

The Cambridge Study in Delinquent Development which began in the 1960s grew in prominence as issues of risk factors in offending and recidivism came to the fore (Farrington et al., 2006). Borrowing from a public health perspective, the risk factor prevention paradigm became highly influential (Farrington et al., 2016). There were critics of what appeared to be problems with risk factors which was a top-down unquestioning about the causal nature of risk factor influence on criminality (Case and Haines, 2015). Risk factors were also a core component of the interventions that youth justice workers operated with, and young people were increasingly perceived as 'posing a risk' or of being 'at risk' of partaking in criminal behaviour (Briggs, 2013).

The Crime and Disorder Act led to the creation of the Youth Justice Board (YJB), which was – and continues – to oversee the administration of youth justice in England and Wales. The Crime and Disorder Act established Youth Offending Teams (YOTs), multi-agency teams which were set up to address offending behaviour by young people in England and Wales, governed by the YJB.[4] At its commencement, the main aim of the YJB was to prevent offending among under-18s (Pitts, 2001); however, more recently, the YJB has been aiming to pursue a 'Child First, Offender Second' approach (Case and Haines, 2016). The principle includes the prioritisation of the best interests of children and pursuing the development of a child's 'pro-social identity for sustainable desistance from crime' (Ministry of Justice/Youth Justice Board (2019, p. 6); all of which should minimise the criminogenic stigma which arises when a child is involved in the youth justice system. Despite this, there remains a focus on 'offender' as the principle aim of YOTs is still to prevent offending (Day, 2022). The fact remains that many guidance documents and frameworks for those working with children and young people in conflict with the law continue to focus on risk and offences rather than children's needs. However, it is important to note that the growing importance of desistance in the National Standards for children in the Youth Justice System, for example, the word 'desistance' is used numerous times, but did not have even one mention in the 2013 version (Bateman, 2020).

The need to expand children's social capital and the provision of legitimate opportunities for taking part in the adult world when they have been in conflict with the law as children is extremely important. These opportunities, within the Youth Justice System are often provide by voluntary organisations (the Third Sector). This will be returned to shortly.

The youth justice system

One role of the YJB is overseeing where children are placed in the juvenile secure estate once they are sentenced by the court. The establishment that children are housed in is dependent on issues such as their age and the

severity of crime. Bearing in mind that the minimum age of criminal responsibility in England and Wales is just 10 years of age (Brown and Charles,
2019), younger children are housed in local government secure children's
homes; some children are contained in privately run secure training centres
and the majority are incarcerated in Young Offenders Institutions (YOIs)
(Price and Turner, 2022).

Provision of services within the secure estate and interventions in the
community associated with the youth justice system are provided by the
state, private organisations, and also by the Third Sector. There are thou-
sands of voluntary organisations working in the criminal justice system,
providing a variety of services and support, and although the provision by
the penal voluntary sector is not without issue (Corcoran et al., 2018), prison-
based programmes can allow for time in spaces that facilitate pro-social
relationships (Abrams et al., 2019). However, sustained and meaningful
involvement by the voluntary sector in the youth justice system in England
and Wales (and elsewhere) is threatened by issues of funding. This is often
connected to a risk-factor based 'payment by results' which can be particularly marginalising for arts-based intentions as it can be more difficult to
quantify impact (Simpson et al., 2019).

However, the positive effects of the arts in prison are long-established,
with studies showing that interventions can improve safety and well-being
in prison and support the process of desistance (Cheliotis, 2014; Gussak,
2006). Generally, access to the arts and culture in prison is perceived as
being cost effective in reducing costs within the criminal justice system and
increases the opportunities for employment among people with convictions
(Plant and Dixon, 2019).

Music in prisons and desistance

Music-making, and in particular singing, was recognised as part of the therapeutic process in prisons during the later 19th and early 20th century (Lee,
2010). Recent years have seen a rise in research on music within prisons
and interest in music as an educational opportunity as well as a therapeutic
activity (Cox and Gelsthorpe, 2008; Digard et al., 2007). Research by the
Prison Reform Trust (PRT) found that music projects were very popular
with prisoners but were not always available.

> Music was the course most desired, and least provided. Prisoners
> praised the music courses they had had at other prisons, and longed to
> have another chance
>
> (Prison Reform Trust, 2003, p. 30)

Music and art programmes offer participants a creative outlet and have a
positive impact on offenders, not least by encouraging them to engage with
further learning and education. Anderson and Overy (2010) for example,

found that engagement in group musical activities within Scottish young offenders' institutions increased young people's engagement in other education programmes after the music project. Research studies have highlighted the relationship between musical development and the development of attributes related to the desistance process (Cursley, 2015).

Desistance

In simple terms, desistance is about an individual stopping offending, although as Wigzell (2021) identifies, there is debate about how this term should be conceptualised. Maruna (2001) describes desistance is the process by which people who have offended stop offending, then continue with a non-offending lifestyle, known as secondary desistance. The key themes of desistance and effective interventions can be grouped into individual dynamics, such as the development of identity, improving personal relationships and providing motivation and hope; and social factors such as improving professional relationships, strengthening social capital and developing new skills (Maruna and LeBel, 2010; Shapland et al., 2016; Wigzell, 2021). These central themes emerge from the literature on musical learning in criminal justice systems (Cox and Gelsthorpe, 2008). The development and maintenance of relationships with professionals and peers, the development of personal as well as social strengths, self-respect and renewed relationships with communities can all be found in the evaluations of music projects. Cursley (2015) suggests that the creative process has similarities to the journey towards desistance because both can offer a person facing challenging issues the hope of progress, and how success and validation can foster optimism, which is a key component of the desistance journey.

Musical learning can arise from shared learning processes which develops the attributes essential for inspiring desistance from crime. Performance of music may act as a catalyst for both preservation and development of social identity. The desistance paradigm centres on changing a criminal identity through the development of social and personal attributes, which resonates with recent research on the transformative effects of music and how musical identity can be changed positively through active and successful music-making (Henley, 2014).

Music in the community and desistance

Projects that divert young people from criminal activity and encourage desistance by using music in the community have been widely evaluated (Daykin et al., 2013). One example is research conducted by Caulfield et al. (2022) with a music programme run by YOT in the Midlands of England. The aim of the programme was to develop the creative, expressive and musical ability of children and young people; improve their confidence and well-being; and improve the level of compliance and successful completion of court orders among project participants. Any child who was in contact with the YOT was allowed to join the project, and the music programme then formed part of the child's individualised sentence plan. 'Measuring' 'success' is always difficult in these (and any similar intervention) and in this study, attendance at YOT appointments was used as a proxy for compliance. This data was compared with similarly matched YOT attending young people who were not part of a music programme. The research found that there was a statistically significant higher level of attendance in those who completed the music project compared to those who had not. Other findings from the study were that young people reported a significant difference in self-reported musical ability following the programme and an improvement in well-being scores after completing the intervention. Qualitative research conducted as part of the project supported quantitative findings with semi-structured interviews from 23 children identifying five themes that were improved by their participation in the project: confidence; professional and social skills; achievements, engagement and aspirations; well-being; and relationships with staff (Caulfield et al., 2022).

Participation in creative programmes has been shown to reduce risk factors and increase protective factors for mental health and well-being, including social support (Cursley and Maruna, 2015), with social barriers broken down in the spaces created in arts programmes leading to improvements in mental health and well-being (Caulfield et al., 2016). The Good Vibrations project, provided by the music charity – the Firebird Trust, involved both prisoners and prison staff, and better relationships between prisoners and staff was an important outcome of the project. The project also reported an improvement in the social skills of those who had participated on the project, and a reduction in anxiety. Staff also reported that prisoners were experiencing less boredom and an increase in desire to change (Wilson et al., 2009).

Linking the carceral and the community

One problem that researchers have identified are issues of fragmentation, when an arts-based project which an individual begins while incarcerated does not continue in the community. When out of prison, it can be difficult to find any continuity with those arts tutors who have encouraged and validated their previous progress. The work of Changing Tunes allowed former offender participants the opportunity to continue their music sessions outside prison (Cursley and Maruna, 2015). One aspect of desistance that is difficult is changes in self-identity, identifying with roles that are not connected to offending, and one important aspect of this project was how many participants identified themselves as musicians rather than offenders.

Putting in place interventions both in and out of prison to enable the desistance journey is multi-faceted – the aim being to lead to the permanence of secondary desistance, where the person no longer thinks of themselves as an offender – rather than primary desistance which refers to a period of non-offending (Maruna and Farrall, 2004). Following release, Changing Tunes participants are invited to remain involved with the organisation through concerts in the community, continuing music sessions and pastoral support as part of a commitment to a 'through the gate' model of change.

Sound connections: Music projects that work with young people

Daykin et al. (2013) conducted a systematic review of 63 papers exploring music projects with young people in contact with the criminal justice system. Their findings suggested that when professional musicians lead music-making, this can be a personal and collective resource for young people. An important aspect of this is that programmes delivered by professional musicians indicate that these people have the skills and experience to garner respect from young people, particularly groups that are difficult to engage and those who present with challenging attitudes and behaviours (De Viggiani et al., 2013). The next section consists of an edited interview between the two authors, focusing on the youth projects provided by professional musician Justin Boreland.[5]

ELEANOR PETERS (EP): Could you tell me about what it is that you do and the kinds of projects that you've been running?

JUSTIN BORELAND (JB): In one project in [a south of England] YOI, I was hired as a music professional to teach music technology on a particular programme and after that particular course we did go on to develop two new courses which are now available to students between the age of 15 and 18 across the country, nationally recognised by [government department] the Education and Skills Funding Agency (ESFA). The music programmes that were available when I joined were quite outdated and tended to be geared towards someone in a band, someone who had some kind of music education or maybe playing instruments, rather than what the young people I have worked with who are more gifted toward the lyrical, song writing or producing.

EP: I worked in [a south of England] YOI many years ago and found it a difficult environment, how have you found working there?

JB: It is a difficult place to work in, you know, it can be difficult to command the respect of the group, but I remember my group was very very organsied very respectful, I only had a couple of issues. They were generally very well behaved, very manageable, very respectful because I suppose, certainly the fact that I'm teaching music, but also they knew that I genuinely cared about them, about them completing their work and that I would go above and beyond what we need to work with them.

EP: Have there been many challenges?

JB: There have been some issues with what music is allowed and what music isn't allowed and there were some big problems with that. That is one of the reasons that I am not there now. It got to a point where it became for me, that it was no longer a music programme, it was where the young people were not allowed to express anything. For example, drill music. There are all sorts of drill music now, but the young people weren't allowed any drill music and then it became kind of grime because the prison didn't know the difference but that is the type of music they listen to. The prison had some rules which I thought were draconian rules, such as that anybody who swears should be instantly taken of the microphone and not allowed to engage in any further type of work. It could be a slip-up - sometimes they don't know any better. What I thought is that we could educate the young people that those words were offensive or inadequate, and inappropriate. We could change them out rearrange, go back and see where those points in the work might be offensive. And that means that the young person has come out with a piece of work that is not offensive, ready for commercial consumption, but also something they can be proud of and it's about where you're coming from.

So, the rules were stifling that expression, and I didn't like it. The situation was often hostile because the young people didn't always understand that what they were saying was something bad or very insulting. Some language would instantly be deemed as hostile, and given that a lot of young people really opened up – dead friends, mom's got a drug problem situation – all these kind of different kinds of topics that they come up with, but they were honest frank and forthright, and I think you should be able to express yourselves up to an extent in that sort of an environment but it became so restricted by rules and conditions that I felt I could no longer do my job.

We had the highest ever rate of exam completion, 96 percent, however, in my first year there over a 100 students who completed their work and then security came in and took their work away. Many of the students had never engaged in academic work in their lives, and they were looking forward to getting good grades, you're working on a project, working towards an exam and you know, someone's taken it away from you.

EP: You said earlier that you had to stop many projects because of COVID, I think that I can imagine how for those young people in YOIs and STCs, that they've had very lonely time without input from organisations like yours.

JB: I've heard a lot from friends I've got still working inside the YOI and they told me that the young people really miss the music workshops; it's therapeutic for them, just trying to be creative and make a difference doing something they really enjoy while they are in a place that they really don't enjoy. It can be very liberating, but unfortunately it is down to [prison] priorities, and that kind of subject hasn't been prioritised lately, but the victims of these policies and the situation are the young people and I feel very, very sorry for them. This is something positive - you've got positive role models in the facilitators. Music can be useful socially as many young people are quite shy of opening up socially, but they can express themselves with music and lyrics. Additionally, some people found a place of sanctuary where they could actually log trauma that they had gone through - they could write and talk about it, in a musical way and get it off their chest, but it is definitely beneficial to all of the students I met.

EP: You also do work in the community, could you tell me about those projects?

JB: We do workshops and recruit students from PRU [pupil referral units] and a programme that we deliver through rock school, which leads to RSL qualifications (https://www.rslawards.com/rockschool/). We take at-risk youth, students who have SEN [special education needs], usually for behavioural difficulties or some kinds of challenges. We deliver this at a lovely art school, and the programme is open to young people across London, aged between 15 to 18.

I also teach at the Institute of Contemporary Music Performance (ICMP) which provides a higher level of qualification, going up to degree level and we have created a career pathway from the community projects which are delivered at levels one to three, straight into ICMP into level 4[6] and beyond. We take a quota of students so they can gain a B.A. [Bachelor of Arts degree] in music, creative composition or digital music production. We're all about trying to find or create a platform for higher education for young people, particularly SEN or those with challenging behaviour, at-risk students in general.

We noted that there were no programmes at degree level; they were all levels 2 and 3 but we were already trying to get the participants to go higher. They're going to be secure, and people will find some kind of employment somewhere because they've got the accreditation and higher education – our projects are closing the gap. We do emphasise that although 90% [of participants] will aspire to be a great pop star, most of us won't, but if we can find a career in the thing that we love we haven't done badly at all.

EP: Research indicates the importance of through-care [services to prisoners both during and after their sentences] - do you have work that connects the community and the prison provision?

JB: We have delivered a successful pilot project which has now been contracted to run on a regular basis. This is a recidivism prevention project where the participants are provided with a music and media project within 3 month of release and this continues 6 months after release, providing them with further academic work and career opportunities for apprenticeships or interviews. The project also helps to develop any material that they have and provide mentoring support. This project worked with 8 of their most persistent reoffenders and 18 months has gone by and to my knowledge, none of them had reoffended.

EP: Can you tell me about the type of music the young people want to play?

JB: The young people like anything from the pop scene, Dua Lipa, the Weeknd, Drake, pop, down to a little more hardcore to R&B, it's a load of different stuff, not all of them are into drill. Certainly, when they go out and normally when they're partying, it'll be a combination of music. But every single, I think genre right now, the lyrics from what they're talking about are normally geared towards either making it, living the fast life or kind of surface level, topics which don't allow or promote any kind of, you know, more serious conversation about what's going on in the world. Not how you might better yourself, do you get what, get what you want at anybody's expense.

Some young people came to the project wanting to engage through drill music, and there were some problems with that particular aspect of teaching. What I said was that it is okay to speak about your experience and what you've been through, but just not in a way that would be offensive to others. You don't need to use swear words away or certain kinds of expressions in order to get yourself across, there are other ways that you can get yourself across.

We just say imagine that it's for radio and you know what radio is like, if you're going to talk about your life or things that happen, it's not always pleasant to hear but it has to be framed in such a way that it's not offensive or endorsing or promoting a lifestyle that's regressive to all of us. They were dealing with the things you see on the news, and they could be some of the most challenging young people, but it was a pleasure working with them and seeing how music as a medium can be therapeutic.

EP: Could you talk me through the positives of using music in these projects?

JB: Music as a medium can be therapeutic, so therapeutic, beneficial for young people and for their well-being in general, and for positive relationships, well-being, self-esteem. The projects can show them a different way - that you can make a living out of something you love and sending that message, that you don't have to re-offend.

It is sad if someone's written off at 16 17, I think it's just, you know, the wrong thing to do. People make mistakes start, but also, I think, as you say, with the joint enterprise, the fact is that people live in an environment where you've got to almost be seen to have allegiance to some of the people just because they live on your street, and you've got to go past them when you go anywhere.

I was rapping at 16, had lots of money, had friends getting mixed up in silly things but nothing that serious that would get you locked up indefinitely. But for the grace of God, it could have been me for a long time because now you've got these new laws and I went out with them [joint enterprise], doing something like a robbery or even worse maybe GBH or murder, and you happened to be with them... You can get the same time as them if they consider that you were part of the conspiracy itself.

EP: You are obviously a huge role model for the young people with your music career and success as a writer, performer and producer. How do you think this helps?

JB: We are just trying to give them avenues and pathways and demonstrations for real life, examples like myself, and bringing in artists and entrepreneurs and other people that can let young people know that people who have been through what you've been through can make the right decisions and come out the other in a better position to really engage and enjoy life in the community. I aim to be a relatable role model myself as a black guy. I was actually in [same YOI] for 3 months when I was 16, they let me out to do Top of the Pops[7], so [I went] from a resident to a teacher. Now I am doing something and teaching something that the young people can relate to and see I have been working in the industry. Maybe they'll look and think, 'you know what, I could do something like Justin does, he does something. I wouldn't mind doing that. You know, he's getting paid alright, he's making music, he's in the music industry'. I always let them know that the mistakes in the past don't necessarily have to define your future. I've also taken my law degree, there's a number of different aspects of my life that they can hopefully look at and take some positivity from.

Conclusion

Desistance is essentially an absence of certain behaviour (Hampson, 2018). It can be seen as a 'life stage' whereby stability, through growing older and maturing, finding a partner or a job signifies the ending of criminal behaviours. It can also be understood as a process where changes in behaviours and identities are formed, and the shift in personal identity was key to Maruna's (2001) understanding of desistance.

The importance of the desistance approach cannot be overstated when considered alongside the other judicial approaches; the retribution' type of 'just desserts', sentencing young people to 'short, sharp, shock' punitive imprisonments, the rise of individualist 'risk factor' analyses allowing for net widening and net thinning to go unbounded (Cohen, 1985). Young people 'posing a risk' or of being 'at risk' of partaking in criminal behaviour which justifies often misplaced early interventions leading to recidivism (Briggs, 2013).

As this chapter has shown, a number of studies have found different benefits through general arts-based participation for those who are incarcerated – these individual benefits include increased well-being, decreased anger, a reduction in incidents of self-harm and aggression and lower anxiety levels. Additionally, there are wider benefits such as projects having a positive impact on the institutional climates of prisons and the positive influence of role models in their peers and the project facilitators. It is the development and maintenance of relationships with professionals and peers that appear the most fruitful of recommendations of using this approach. Evaluations of music projects have found that they can help with the development of personal growth, but importantly can build social, communal strengths. One issue that studies have found is that the transient nature of the prison population can lead to issues of fragmentation. Severed relationships with the tutors who encouraged and validated their previous progress can be problematic for the person's positive well-being and morale; therefore, the ability to continue projects begun within the prison walls out into the community is imperative (De Viggiani et al., 2013).

Music can have important cultural resonance for young people in contact with criminal justice system, who may find it difficult or personally challenging to express themselves through conventional or expected channels. Engagement via participation in music may reach people in ways mainstream programmes of education, healthcare or rehabilitation fail. A child who has been in conflict with the law, particularly, needs help to expand their social capital and the provision of legitimate opportunities for taking part in the adult world – we cannot write young people off. The success of projects such as the ones identified in this chapter should be encouraged. For example, Boreland's projects show what a positive role model, someone they can relate to in terms of background and experience, someone they can look up in an aspirational way, modelling the positive and showing how a passion for music can be an identity, an occupation, but most importantly a hopeful future.

Notes

1 In 1908 the Children Act established a separate court for young people dealing with both crime and welfare needs.
2 Arguably these were an early form of diversion and rehabilitation, although a focus on being a moral useful citizen could be seen as coercive (Gear, 1999).
3 Although these two approaches are often both in play to differing degrees at the same time (Goldson, 2005).
4 The Youth Justice Board are responsible for children in conflict with the law in; out of court disposals; representing children at court; supervising and monitoring community court disposals; accommodating children in secure settings; and the transitional and resettlement of young people (MoJ/YJB, 2019).
5 Justin, PKA Merlin, a rapper, producer and educator, joined a group called Bomb the Bass at the age of 16 and getting signed by the iconic US label Sire Records (Madonna, Ice-T) just a year later. Justin's production and song writing talents have led him to be involved in more than 20 UK top 20 hits and he has also spent much of his career working on educational initiatives for at-risk youth and ex-offenders.
6 In England, Wales and Northern Ireland, there are eight different levels of education, level one consists of GCSEs and some NVQs; AS levels, A levels and higher NVQs are level 3; level 4 acts as the bridge between level 3 and 5, and can help people progress to the next stage of education when they might not have

been able to with their previous qualifications, level 6 is a Bachelor's degree while level 8 is PhD (https://www.gov.uk/what-different-qualification-levels-mean/list-of-qualification-levels).

7 Top of the Pops, the UK's flagship music programme which ran on BBC 1964 to 2006.

References

Abrams, L.S., Moreno, M. and Harrikari, T. (2019) The Voluntary Sector Role in Youth and Young Adult Justice Services: A Comparative Case Study of Finland and England/Wales. *Youth Justice*, 19 (3); 278–298.

Anderson, K. and Overy, K. (2010) Engaging Scottish Young Offenders in Education through Music and Art. *International Journal of Community Music*, 3(1); 47–64.

Bateman, T. (2020) *The State of Youth Justice 2020: An Overview of Trends and Developments.* London: NAYJ.

Bateman, T. and Hazel, N. (2022) *Youth Justice Timeline* – Beyond Youth Custody. Youth justice timeline - Beyond Youth Custody. Retrieved from http://www.beyondyouthcustody.net/resources/publications/youth-justice-timeline/

Briggs, D.B. (2013) Conceptualising Risk and Need: The Rise of Actuarialism and the Death of Welfare? Practitioner Assessment and Intervention in the Youth Offending Service. *Youth Justice,* 13 (1); 17–30.

Brown, A. and Charles, A. (2019) The Minimum Age of Criminal Responsibility: The Need for a Holistic Approach. *Youth Justice*, 21 (2); 153–171.

Case, S. and Haines, K. (2015) *Positive Youth Justice: Children First, Offenders Second.* Bristol: Policy Press.

Case, S. and Haines K. (2016) Taking the Risk out of Youth Culture. In Trotter, C., McIvor, G. and McNeill, F. (Eds.) *Beyond the Risk Paradigm in Criminal Justice*, pp. 61–75. London: Palgrave Macmillan.

Caulfield, L., Jolly, A., Simpson, E. and Devi-McGleish, Y. (2022) 'It's Not Just Music, It Helps You from Inside': Mixing Methods to Understand the Impact of Music on Young People in Contact with the Criminal Justice System. *Youth Justice*, 22 (1); 67–84.

Caulfield, L.S., Wilkinson, D.J. and Wilson, D. (2016) Exploring Alternative Terrain in the Rehabilitation and Treatment of Offenders: Findings from a Prison-Based Music Project. *Journal of Offender Rehabilitation*, 55 (6); 396–418.

Cheliotis, L. (2014) *The Arts of Desistance: Evaluation of the Koestler Trust Arts Mentoring Programme for Former Prisoners.* London: London School of Economics and Political Science.

Cohen, S. (1985) *Visions of Social Control.* Cambridge: Polity Press.

Corcoran, M.S., Williams, K., Prince, M. and Maguire, M. (2018) The Penal Voluntary Sector in England and Wales: Adaptation to Unsettlement and Austerity. *The Political Quarterly*, 89 (2); 187–196.

Cox, P. (2017) Borstals. In Turner, J., Taylor, P., Corteen, K. and Morley, S. (Eds.) *A Companion to the History of Crime and Criminal Justice*, pp. 16–18. Bristol: Policy Press.

Cox, A. and Gelsthorpe, L. (2008) *Beats and Bars, Music in Prison: An Evaluation.* Cambridge: Institute of Criminology.

Cursley, J. (2015) *Time for an Encore: Exploring the Symbiotic Links between Music, Forming Meaningful Relationships and Desistance.* Papers from the British Criminology Conference, 15; 7–25.

Cursley, J. and Maruna, S. (2015) *A Narrative-Based Evaluation of 'Changing Tunes' Music-Based Prisoner Reintegration Interventions.* London: Paul Hamlin Trust.

Day, A. (2022) 'It's a Hard Balance to Find': The Perspectives of Youth Justice Practitioners in England on the Place of 'Risk' in an Emerging 'Child-First' World. *Youth Justice.* https://doi.org/10.1177/14732254221075205

Daykin, N., De Viggiani, N., Pilkington, P. and Moriaty, Y. (2013) Music Making for Health, Well-Being and Behaviour Change in Youth Justice Settings: A Systematic Review. *Health Promotion International*, 28 (2); 197–210.

De Viggiani, N., Daykin, N., Moriarty, Y. and Pilkington, P. (2013) *Musical Pathways: An Exploratory Study of Young People in the Criminal Justice System, Engaged with a Creative Music Programme.* Bristol: DHSS/UWE.

Digard, L., von Sponeck, A. and Liebling, A. (2007) All Together Now: The Therapeutic Potential of a Prison-Based Music Programme. *Prison Service Journal*, 170; 3–14.

Farrington, D., Coid, J., Harnett, L., Jolliffe, D., Soteriou, N., Turner, R. and West, D. (2006) *Criminal Careers up to Age 50 and Life Success up to Age 48: New Findings from the Cambridge Study in Delinquent Development.* Home Office Research Study 299.

Farrington, D.P., Ttofia, M.M. and Piquero, A.R. (2016) Risk, Promotive, and Protective Factors in Youth Offending: Results from the Cambridge Study in Delinquent Development. *Journal of Criminal Justice*, 45; 63–70.

Field, E. (1969) Research into Detention Centres. *The British Journal of Criminology,* 9 (1); 62–71.

Gear, G. (1999) *Industrial Schools in England, 1857–1933 'Moral Hospitals' or 'Oppressive Institutions'?* A thesis submitted in fulfilment of the requirements for the degree of Doctor of Philosophy, University of London Institute of Education.

Goldson, B. (2005) Taking Liberties: Policy and the Punitive Turn. In H. Hendrick (Ed.) *Children and Social Policy: An Essential Reader*, pp. 225–267. Bristol: The Policy Press.

Gussak, D. (2006) The Effects of Art Therapy with Prison Inmates: A Follow-Up Study. *Arts in Psychotherapy*, 33; 188–198.

Hampson, K.S. (2018) Desistance Approaches in Youth Justice – The Next Passing Fad or a Sea-Change for the Positive? *Youth Justice*, 18 (1); 18–33.

Henley, J. (2014) Musical Learning and Desistance from Crime: The Case of a 'Good Vibrations' Javanese Gamelan Project with Young Offenders. *Music Education Research*, 17 (1); 103–120.

Lee, R. (2010) Music Education in Prisons: A Historical Overview. *International Journal of Community Music*, 3 (1); 7–18.

Maruna, S. (2001) *Making Good: How Ex-Convicts Reform and Rebuild Their Lives.* Washington: American Psychological Association.

Maruna, S. and Farrall, S. (2004) Desistance from Crime: A Theoretical Reformulation. *olner Zeitschrift fur Soziologie und Sozialpsychologie*, 43; 171–194.

Maruna, S. and LeBel, T. (2010) The Desistance Paradigm in Correctional Practice: From Programmes to Lives. In F. McNeill, P. Raynor and C. Trotter (Eds.) *Offender Supervision: New Directions in Theory, Research and Practice.* Oxon: Willan Publishing.

Menis, S. (2012) More Insights on the English Borstal: 'Shaping' or Just 'Shaking' the Young-Offender? *International Journal of Criminology and Sociological Theory*, 5 (3); 985–998.

Ministry of Justice/Youth Justice Board (2019) *Standards for Children in the Youth Justice System 2019*. London: HMSO. Retrieved from https://assets.publishing. service.gov.uk/government/uploads/system/uploads/attachment_data/file/78 0504/Standards_for_children_in_youth_justice_services_2019.doc.pdf.

Muncie, J. (2008) The `Punitive Turn' in Juvenile Justice: Cultures of Control and Rights Compliance in Western Europe and the USA. *Youth Justice*, 8 (2); 107–121.

Nash, M. and Savage, S.P. (1995) Criminal Justice Managers: Setting Targets or Becoming Targeted? *International Journal of Public Sector Management*, 8 (1); 4–10.

Pitts, J. (2001) Korrectional Karaoke: New Labour and the Zombification of Youth Justice. *Youth Justice*, 1 (2); 3–16.

Plant, J. and Dixon, D. (2019) *Enhancing Arts and Culture in the Criminal Justice System: A Partnership Approach*. London: National Criminal Justice Arts Alliance.

Price, J. and Turner, J. (2022) (Custodial) Spaces to Grow? Adolescent Development during Custodial Transitions. *Journal of Youth Studies*, 25 (2); 225–241.

Prison Reform Trust (2002) Time to Learn Prisoners' Views on Prison Education. Retrieved from http://www.prisonreformtrust.org.uk/wp-content/uploads/old_ files/Documents/Time_to_LearnBook.pdf

Shapland, J., Farrall, S. and Bottoms, A. (Eds.) (2016) *Global Perspectives on Desistance: Reviewing What We Know and Looking to the Future*. Abingdon: Routledge.

Shaw, S. (1985) Reflections on 'Short Sharp Shock'. *Youth and Policy: The Journal of Critical Analysis*, 12; 1–5.

Simpson, E., Morgan, C. and Caulfield, L.S. (2019) From the Outside In: Narratives of Creative Arts Practitioners Working in the Criminal Justice System. *The Howard Journal of Criminal Justice*, 58 (3); 384–403.

Wigzell, A. (2021) *Explaining Desistance: Looking Forward, Not Backwards*. NAYJ Briefing.

Wilson, D., Caulfield, L. and Atherton, S. (2009) Good Vibrations: The Long-Term Impact of a Prison-Based Music Project. *Prison Service Journal Issue*, 182; 27–32.

Index

9 781032 030500